IAN GODFREY. Moon Ring.

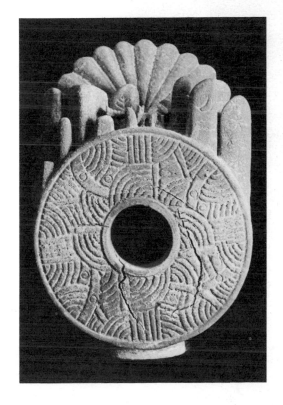

Frontispiece.
DANKA NAPIORKOWSKA
& ROGER MICHELL.
Tiger vase in slip cast earthenware with
silk-screened decoration.

POTTERS
ON
POTTERY

Elisabeth Cameron

Philippa Lewis

Evans Brothers Limited

London

Published by Evans Brothers Limited,
Montague House, Russell Square,
London WC1

First Published 1976

Produced by Carter Nash Cameron Limited,
25 Lloyd Baker Street, London WC1X 9AT.
Set by SX Composing Limited, 61 Oakwood Avenue,
Leigh-on-Sea, Essex.
Printed by Page Bros (Norwich) Limited,
Mile Cross Lane, Norwich NOR 45N.
Bound by Robert Hartnoll Limited, Victoria Square,
Bodmin, Cornwall.
Printed and bound in Great Britain.

ISBN 0 237 44855 6

Designed and photographed by Ian Cameron.

Other photographs by:
Alan Barrett-Danes (pages 8–17)
David Cripps (pages 35, 62, 64, 65, 68, 69)
David Hicks, Charles Benfield and Tom Northey (pages 78–83)
Steve White and Chris Foster (pages 36, 96–101)
George Cummings (page 107)
Michael Holford (page 115)
Design Centre (page 121, bottom)
Eric Webster (pages 127–135)

We are grateful to the following galleries for allowing us
to take photographs during their exhibitions: Casson
Gallery (Michael Casson, Peter Starkey), British Craft Centre
(David Leach), New Grafton Gallery (Siddig A. El'Nigoumi),
Brian Koetser Gallery (Yeap Poh Chap).

Contents

Alan & Ruth Barrett-Danes   8

Svend Bayer   19

Alan Caiger-Smith   30

Michael Cardew   47

Michael Casson   54

Elizabeth Fritsch   62

Ian Godfrey   70

Mo Jupp   78

David Leach   84

Danka Napiorkowska & Roger Michell   96

Bryan Newman   106

Siddig A. El'Nigoumi   118

Mary Rogers   126

Peter Starkey   137

Geoffrey Swindell   144

Yeap Poh Chap   156

Biographies   165

Introduction

Since World War II, it has become a more realistic possibility to make a living as a potter in Britain. There has been a growing demand for studio pottery as an alternative to factory-made ware for everyday use, and at the same time it is no longer regarded as eccentric to collect pots as art objects; the increased interest in ceramics has been accompanied by a sharp rise in the standards expected both by maker and consumer. This remarkable craft revival has been encouraged by the promotion and support of such bodies as the Crafts Advisory Council and the Council for Small Industries in Rural Areas.

An important contribution towards the understanding of pottery and the clarification of the potter's position in industrial society was the work of Bernard Leach, who had returned to England from Japan in 1920. His workshop at St Ives was based on an attitude to the craftsman's role that echoed hopes expressed by William Morris in the late nineteenth century. In many followers throughout England and America, Leach's own pots as well as his writing and teaching inspired a comprehension of the Japanese search for aesthetic values in the whole pot through the craftsman's sympathetic treatment of his material. Those who were successful in combining sensitivity and technical skill have built up a tradition of functional ware of great beauty and character.

A contrasting view of pots as an art form, without regard to any function, had been expressed by William Staite Murray. After experimenting with pottery before World War I, he had derived new inspiration from seeing Shoji Hamada's work in the early 1920s. Staite Murray sold individually titled pots at high prices in fine art galleries, and in 1925 became head of the ceramic department at the Royal College of Art, where he influenced a new generation of potters.

The use of ceramics as a medium for self-expression was mainly restricted to thrown pots, frequently made in stoneware, until the art schools began to move towards hand building. Since then, the number of possibilities has increased until the only factor which determines your choice of style and technique as a potter is your own wish to work in a particular way. You can select from a wide range of proprietary materials whose relative refinement and predictable behaviour allow you to concentrate on the making. On the other hand, you can still prepare your own clay and glazes if you want to experiment with what nature offers. Equally, you can choose to express yourself in a form which has no claim to function other than its own existence, or you can restrict your output to large numbers of identical mugs. Even when traditional or ethnic styles are strictly followed, they are freely chosen.

The potters in this book, all working in Britain, represent a wide variety of approach. They are naturally drawn from those who felt willing to talk to us about their work in spite of the difficulties of expressing in words the conscious and subconscious processes behind the making of their pots.

Each section is the result of one or two tape recorded discussions, which were then pieced together, with our questions omitted. We generally asked about their beginnings as potters, the sources which influence their work, and their technical methods, in order to get some feel of what the whole business of being a potter involves. The text is therefore a combination of subjects brought up by us and any which the potters themselves felt inclined to introduce. While the potters have seen and approved the text, we accept responsibility for any errors in fact or emphasis that may be the result of our editing. Nevertheless, we hope that these interviews will give some indication of the inspirations, aims and methods of the potters we met.

The photographs are intended to provide visual documentation of the potters' work, but it seems important to stress that there can be no substitute for familiarity with the pots themselves through touch as well as sight.

Alan & Ruth Barrett-Danes

Alan and Ruth Barrett-Danes collaborate on fantasy sculptural pieces made in porcelain. Alan is responsible for the basic form and technical aspects of the piece, while Ruth shares in the development of ideas and models the figures and animals. Alan is Senior Lecturer in Ceramics at Cardiff College of Art, and Ruth works as an art therapist in a Cardiff Hospital.

Ruth: It does not seem to me that people need to know what is in our minds when we are working, because I think if you have feeling for what is there, you are going to sense the elements and build into them ideas that interact with your own emotions. Although the work means something rather more specific to Alan and me, it is not so personal that it does not strike chords in other people.

I enjoy working through literary sources. A lot of the subject matter stems from books that I have read over the years, especially *Beowulf,* the Gilgamesh epic, C. S. Lewis's Narnia books, J. R. R. Tolkien, Mervyn Peake, and mythology in general. It is tending to link up with the kind of work that I am involved with in my teaching. This is not to be taken too

Frog-men seated on thrown, lidded bowls. Porcelain with in-glaze lustre.

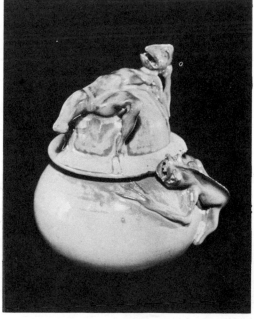

literally, but I am concerned with psychiatric patients—a lot of whom have pent-up emotions which you can sense, though they are unable to communicate through normal channels. You have to find ways through to these inner feelings. Sometimes the patients have such terrible problems that you are in a helpless situation. You feel that there is so much in them that if only you could find the key to let it out, it would be solved. To know that you cannot communicate with people must build up in you terrific tensions, and that enters into it as well. Those are some of the things I am thinking about when I am modelling in clay. I think the pots provide a lovely breathing space. A lot of problems are simplified when you can concentrate on the one aspect.

Alan tries to plan things ahead and I do not. I enjoy drawing, and probably draw a lot around the subject before I begin, but my work is not something which is thought out beforehand. I feel that ideas come through working—what might not necessarily have been a very good idea to start with has to go through the process of working, and from that other things follow. The development from frog to frog-man really occurred through working on the pots and concentrating on the figures.

Alan: When the children were very young, we used to find fungi while walking in the Wenalt area of the Caerphilly Mountains. The children, being on a lower level than adults, discovered all this miniature life among the grass and bracken. We started out by drawing and modelling directly from fungoids—not trying to do anything but translate the forms into ceramic equivalents. I know the toadstool has been used by several other

Fungoid forms modelled in porcelain: sprayed slip and M.O.P. lustre glaze.

potters as a form, but I was thinking of the environmental aspects, and the life systems within the habitats.

At the same time, we were going to Porthcawl, and the long stretch of inter-tidal coastline presented other environmental possibilities. I started to photograph the coast, and also went to the south of France, where I took a lot of slides of prehistoric caves and the environments within them. The theme of Predators started to evolve from the mysteries in the rock tunnels, and the miniature marine life which was quite busily and happily getting on with its living, completely unseen. The coast at Porthcawl is difficult to

Predators: snails (below) and toads (right) in brown glazed fungoid habitats. 1974.

reach even when it is not covered by the tide. I found that it acted as a springboard for ideas, and used to contemplate that kind of environment by looking at slides projected on the wall.

I started making cabbages which were habitats for bodies, creatures. There was a lot of social comment in there, cabbages being symbolic of a utilitarian kind of existence, boring, repetitive, hopeless. Then it seemed that it would be interesting to move the creature inside the cabbage itself— instead of regarding the cabbage as a habitat, turning the cabbage into a person who shows all the symptoms of that way of life. The sad cabbage-head seems to personify the hopelessness of the situation. There are all these nasty crevices, out of which come creatures, who are in fact the memories of people that relate to the head. Because of the hopeless state the subjects find themselves in, frustration builds up, and the thoughts and memories bursting out are their only means of communication.

The transition from head to cabbage is quite intentional because I think of a cabbage as an everyday, mundane thing which is always there, although we tend to dismiss it, and that is why I hope the head is a little late in appearing, you do not quite see it at first.

In making cabbage-heads, I take moulds of leaves. Initially, I used to build up the cabbages with eight or ten leaves in layers, like the real plants.

ALAN & RUTH BARRETT-DANES

Later, they had only five or six leaves arranged around a thrown base—more head than cabbage. I used different kinds of cabbage leaf—Savoy or, for softer, fleshy, less brittle effects, leaves with less pronounced textures. Very consciously, I was aware of the quality of lustre glaze and how it works on an undulating surface, as well as the impact of the whole piece.

Some of the more recent examples are rather unpleasant, because I started to introduce more realistic, less pretty colours which signified bleeding. Possibly I am a bit sadistic, but I think the effects could have become much more grotesque if I had not had strong enough control, a rein to stop at a certain point. When I made eyes that were bleeding, it all became too obvious; I prefer it to be more suggestive. What I am going to do now I have no idea. I have said all I can say through the cabbage-heads; to go on could only be repetitive. I should only be able to invest them with a more potent quality, which would be superficial—just ringing the changes.

I have been wondering whether to move on to saltglaze. I tried some, and the pieces went wild, as my kiln was too fast. I am aware of the attraction of technical achievement, but have to consider whether it is going to help the idea. Everyone goes through a transitional intermediary period

Cabbage-heads modelled in white porcelanic clay; reduced in-glaze lustre. 1975.

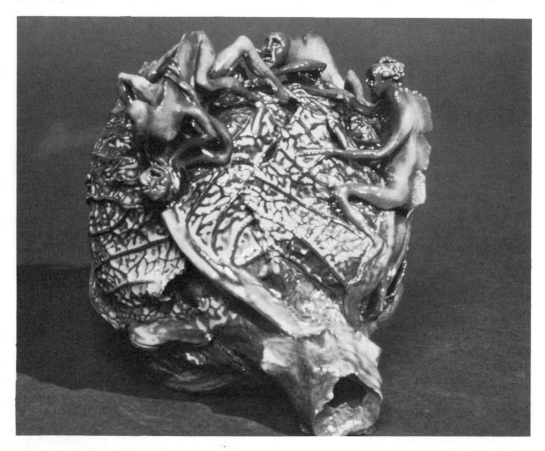

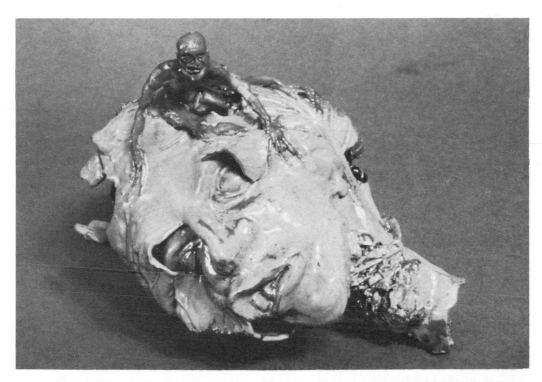

between ideas. When you have done all you can with one, there is a vacuum before you go on to something else. I am making thrown pots at the moment because I have to be doing. It is no good sitting thinking that it will come, for it jolly well won't. The making has got to be directed at an idea. A lot has to be thought around the subject, and then you move into the making slowly, going farther and farther from the original thought, until finally you may have something which has nothing to do with it and throw the work away. Very rarely do you accept it.

I have always worked with clay and, being very conservative, I never stray far from it. In the course of several years spent as an industrial designer in the Potteries before going into teaching, I became interested in the technical problems that arise in a factory, and I think that may be why I like to stay with ceramics. No matter how difficult the question, I like that kind of challenge, the thing between me and the problem. I like the invention in finding a technical solution.

The criticism has been levelled at me, probably rightly, that I tend to build my ideas on information that I have, rather than let the ideas make

Frogs modelled in porcelain on thrown, lidded pots; in-glaze lustre fired at 980°C.

demands on my technical knowledge. For instance, I am very interested in the way inglaze lustre works, I am conscious of the play of light over lustre, and so on. The cabbages have been more successful when the qualities one perceives in the imagery are working *for* the imagery, rather than those which are rather nasty objects which have this interesting surface. There is a very real danger that I might be seduced by the lustre and let it become so powerful that it can actually destroy the idea, but I think this has very much more to do with the idea than the actual quality of the surface. People liked white cabbages until I lustred them, and then they started to think about the lustre effect. Some potters would not touch it because of the associations with Belleek and art deco, but I think those connotations are probably overcome by the shock of seeing the lustre on ten cabbages under fluorescent light in an exhibition case.

Lustre glazes are sprayed on thinly with a lot of air. If you introduce an extra flux and apply a certain thickness of glaze, it will shrink and give you a variegated surface. You can have it cracking or smooth, and it is possible to control it fully. The marvellous thing is that if you do not like the effect you can change it—you can fire it countless times. The reduction that you use lasts only a matter of minutes, so that if you happen to over-reduce and do not like the result, you can re-fire the glaze to change the texture and colour. I do not think many people work like that. The matt black is achieved by smoking—a vanadium oxide, when smoked, goes black, but turns back to green if re-oxidized.

I do a lot of testing on the technical side and I find that a lot of exploration occurs in the area of glazes. It has been a bad influence in cases where I have tried to accomodate the glaze. If you find a good one, you want the world to know about it, and some pieces show evidence of panic—where I have used pigment under some portions to get a change in the glaze, for example. However, I am finding now that, while I am still experimenting, I am more concerned with the synthesis of the whole thing, bringing all the elements together and trying to play a tune of some kind.

We suffer big losses—not through breakage, but in the colour. Although, as I said, you can re-fire the lustre, you can never remove metallic salts once you have applied them—no matter how clean the surface looks, the salts will have migrated into the clay and fire up. Sometimes you make mistakes in the thickness of the spray—you must be very methodical with this kind of surface. I think a lot of studio potters like to restrict themselves to one or two glazes; they like to have it all fairly well under control, they like to know well in advance what this final statement is going to be— a satin finish with a pigment, or whatever. I can understand that. When you are working in my kind of way, it is always a bit chancy.

I think it is a good thing that Ruth and I might sometimes differ in our approach, although it is difficult to work together in some ways, where you are both working on the same piece. There are certain things Ruth is very keen to project that have to be reconciled with other aspects that she tends not to consider, and I get a little concerned about that. I know I think more formally. Ruth's imagination introduces other elements which are sometimes very interesting but impossible to translate. The problem is to find the form that can somehow express what Ruth wants to say. But I insist that it can't be done, and we get this terrible situation which achieves nothing but the release of a lot of nervous tension, when what we really want is something more tangible, some result.

We often discuss what we are trying to do. Ruth says she is not very interested in the technique; once the idea is executed in terms of the modelling, she usually lets me have control of the way I finalize it. What we are always trying to do is to synthesize what Ruth has to offer, and whatever other factors arise. If you can bring it together, you have got something working. That is not always easy to achieve.

Stress. Frog-man, seated on thrown, lidded porcelain pot. 1975.

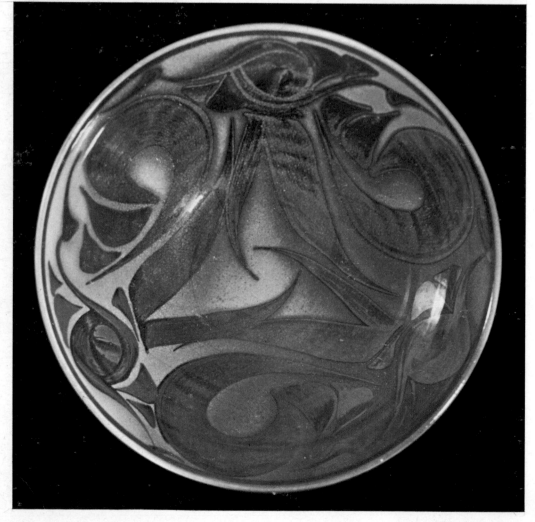

Svend Bayer

Svend Bayer produces functional stoneware at Sheepwash in North Devon. Having worked with Michael Cardew at Wenford Bridge, he set up entirely on his own and built a kiln to his own design, based on some that he saw being used in Korea.

Some of the finest stoneware and porcelain made in the Far East came from Korea. It is rather coarse to look at, not fine in the way Imperial Chinese porcelain is fine, but artistically very pleasing. Today there is still a strong tradition for pottery and the Koreans use stoneware pots in their everyday life—it's the only country I've visited where you can go into a cheap restaurant and be served in stoneware bowls. I can think of one or two expensive places in London, but the little food bowls I am talking about reach standards that most potters would be very glad to attain.

A lot of food in Korea is pickled in large jars, anything up to three feet high. They are beautifully made by a combination of throwing and coiling and have a simple black glaze. The making is as quick as throwing alone and great numbers of these pots are made in a day. The old Korean pots often had turned foot rings, but the ones I saw being made were far less sophisticated, though well enough made for trimming to be unnecessary.

The black glaze contains three parts of a fusible iron-rich clay and one part wood ash; it is very shiny and is most probably not a true stoneware glaze. One of the drawbacks of their kilns was the great difference in temperature between top and bottom. As the heat rises naturally to the top of a kiln, the pots at the bottom were generally underdone—certainly, the older pots quite often look very dull, just a muddy sort of brown with ash on the sides. I think it was found that the shiny pots sold more easily, so they put small quantities of lead in the glaze to ensure that it would melt wherever it was in the kiln.

A long tunnel kiln is used, with a large firebox at one end and a long arch extending some 120 feet up a gentle slope; the pots are stacked, one on top of the other, inside the arch. All the way up the sides are stoke holes about one foot apart. First of all, the firebox end is fired, bringing the first section of the kiln to the desired temperature very slowly over a period of two days, then each successive section is boosted by stoking through the side holes. This part of the firing is extremely rapid. The kiln has a very sound structure and is economical to fire.

ALAN CAIGER-SMITH. Bowl and large dish thrown in tin-glazed earthenware with lustre painting.

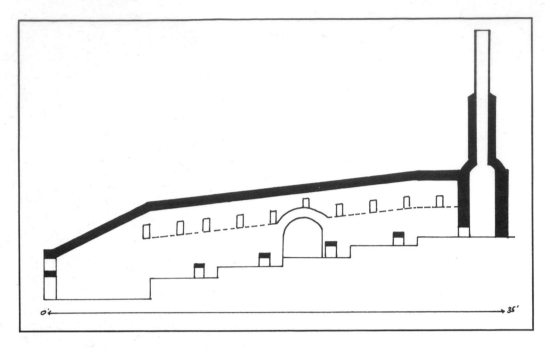

Climbing kiln, based on Korean type, designed by Svend Bayer.

I became great friends with Todd Piker, an American who worked at Wenford Bridge for about a year whilst I was there. He returned to the United States and his father bought a place that they thought they could turn into a pottery. He invited me over to help him, and we built a big wood fired kiln in which we tried to incorporate the structural simplicity of the Korean kilns with the advantages of a more even heat distribution found in the chambered climbing kilns of the Far East. If one can force the draught downwards in a kiln, a more even distribution of heat can be obtained, and we were able to do this by the way in which the pots were stacked in the kiln. The tunnel was divided into five steps, and a row of saggars was arranged at the front of each step to within a foot of the kiln ceiling, forcing the draught upwards from the preceding chamber. Behind, there was the bulk of the setting in larger and more open saggars, and beyond them was a pedestal. Saggars containing pots were placed on this pedestal right up to the ceiling, forcing the draught down under the pedestal into the firebox of the next chamber. There were a pair of stoke holes for each chamber's firebox and another two in the middle of each chamber to boost the temperature at the back of the chamber. The kiln, with a capacity of 600 cubic feet, fired in 20 hours and used only three cords of wood (1 cord = 8ft × 4ft × 4ft), which compared extremely favourably with other wood fired kilns I had used or seen in action.

Glazes do not hold a great fascination for me; the most interesting thing is throwing pots. That is what I find most satisfying, and once the pot leaves the wheel I really begin to lose interest, but I very much enjoyed firing the

Jar glazed with slip (75% iron rich clay, 25% wood ash); roller decoration.

kiln that I built because, unlike many kilns, the stoke holes enabled you to see what was going on inside. When you stoke, you open up a stoke hole to throw a load of wood in, and you can peep in for a few seconds—actually that's about as much as you can stand because of the intensity of fire-light and heat. When you throw the wood in, the temperature drops as it begins to ignite. The colour is a dirty red or orange, and you cannot make anything out distinctly because there is a lot of carbon burning all round the pots. Then, when it is really burning well and getting enough oxygen, the temperature rises and suddenly the whole thing clears up with very ghostly whisps of turquoise, blue and white. That is at top temperature. Most potters try to reduce their pots, mainly for clay and glaze colour. I only fired that kiln three times, because I knew that I would be leaving America and I wanted to get as many firings in as possible. But with a kiln like that, you have to fire it many times before you begin to get much control over it.

When I went to Wenford Bridge, I had not done any pottery, so obviously whilst I was there I was copying what Michael Cardew was making. That's the way I learnt. He had just returned from Australia and was working alone when I wrote to him; I was very fortunate. Probably, the reason I was later so attracted to Korean pots was that I could identify with them. Michael Cardew drew much of his inspiration from the North Devon Potteries, especially Fremington, and the basic shapes of the pans and jars in Korea are very similar to theirs, very straightforward. Koreans are the only Far Eastern potters I saw who made pulled handles, the sort used in North Devon. But I suppose that another reason I liked them was that they seemed like a breath of fresh air after Japan.

In Japan, it was very much like the West. Although there are a great many potteries, there didn't seem to be many traditional potters in the Korean sense. Also they are very precious about their pots. People in Japan are prepared to pay very high prices for pots, which are considered to be

works of art, not so much household utensils, although to be fair, a great deal of domestic pottery is made too. In Korea that attitude does not exist. The vast majority of pots are made by people who do not consider them anything special, although they are very beautiful.

It may be the result of the early tea masters in Japan, who first realised that a lot of rough peasant pottery was beautiful. Ever since, it would seem the Japanese have been trying consciously to imitate something which by its very nature cannot be imitated. What was so good about the early rice bowls was that they were made by very poor people who had to make hundreds and thousands of them in order to survive. They were very casual and spontaneous in the way they made them and there is something very beautiful about that, but to set out to copy it is a contradiction in terms.

I was at one of the old Japanese pottery centres, looking around a show-room, and the thing I liked best was a small pot, about six inches tall, just a little storage jar without a lid. It had been fired in the open and had a fairly heavy ash deposit down one side. That pot cost $200. That is not pottery, at least not as far as I am concerned because everything bar the throwing

Casserole and teapot, both with iron slip glaze, made at Wenford Bridge. Teapot coloured by ash during firing.

was totally accidental and gratuitous. Why should the potter pat himself on the back for the fire's spontaneity, and anyway who needs a $200 storage jar?

I think there is a tendency in England for potters to start out too timidly. They are often prepared to spend quite substantial amounts of money on small electric kilns, gas kilns, electric or manufactured wheels, none of them cheap to buy, and often expensive to run. I would prefer to build my own wheel and try to make it fit me and to build my own large kiln, since large kilns are more economical than small ones. To produce many pots does not vastly increase your material costs. Take the two kilns that I have worked with, one with a capacity of about 120 cubic feet, the other 600

Casserole, baking dish, and tea and coffee pots, made at Wenford Bridge, all in stoneware with iron slip glazes, in the case of the coffee pot over white slip.

Jug with clay and ash glaze down to shoulder; covered jar, Albany slip glaze with zircon slip trailing; (opposite) unglazed candlestick. All stoneware, made (1974) in America.

cubic feet—on average the larger produces five times as many pots by weight each firing than the smaller kiln, in two thirds of the time and using slightly more than half the amount of wood. This means that, pot for pot, it is ten times as efficient in its use of wood and eight times as efficient in time taken to fire. The bigger kiln also means a saving in time spent packing and unpacking and repairs since firings are not so frequent.

I think that making large numbers of pots is important. If you make too few, there is a risk that they may become overloaded with whatever it is that you put into them. Making too many can also have a bad effect—it can mean that you begin to cut corners and your work can become slovenly and numbers become more important than the pots themselves—but within reason it is very good for you. It means that you do not overdecorate, you do not make terribly complicated shapes or add a lot of useless embellishments. You simply have not time for that. Also there is the economic consideration: the more pots you make, the more competitive you can make your prices.

There were only two of us at the pottery in Connecticut. We were working very hard. We had only been at it for a few months and most of that was spent building and making refractories. We had actually been making pots for three months and I think that perhaps after a year we would have got into a kind of rhythm where the work would have become less and less strenuous. After I left the idea was to find someone else. I think it is hard to take on someone because potters are usually working on a fairly small margin and they cannot really afford to pay wages. You have to be very well organized to pay wages and, generally speaking, many people who set out to be potters are a bit on the romantic side and such practical matters don't come easily. I do not really care for the practicalities but they are important and if you have your feet firmly on the ground you are less likely to make unnecessary mistakes. In the same way, a knowledge of physics and chemistry enables you to make educated guesses. In North America, and England too, the materials that are used, unless you go out and dig your own, have mainly been analysed and, provided you understand the basics, what happens is fairly predictable.

In New England, some selling goes on at the big trade and craft fairs. Potters have in some cases to submit work to enter, but once in they derive enormous advantages from the opportunity to show their pots to a very large number of potential buyers. These fairs made a lot of sense to me, especially for someone with a big kiln. Ours produced on average 800 largish pots a firing, and our main concern was to move them as quickly as possible—there is nothing more depressing than being inundated with unsold pots. Going round from shop to shop with pots is an unsatisfactory and very expensive way of selling. Often small shops will not handle large numbers of pots. On the contrary, they often encourage potters to go the other way, to make small numbers of highly artistic (and I do not care for that word in this context) pots.

SVEND BAYER

The difficult thing in North America is that the tradition for pottery, though once very strong, has died and consequently people do not know how to use pots. To them pottery is a few names—Scandinavian or Finnish stoneware and porcelain. In England you can make a lot of things like colanders, for example, and sell them, but in America people would not know what to do with them. There is some conscientous revival of pottery, but unfortunately most of us are not content to make just good straight-forward pots. Many pots that you see around are gimmicky, and that's partly the potter's fault and partly the public's fault. Potters think they ought to do something a bit special, and special can mean anything.

I worked at a pottery factory at Barnstaple for six months just after I left Wenford Bridge. They make flower pots, garden pots and a little domestic ware, some of which is slip decorated. I mainly made pitchers, storage jars and strawberry pots. Whilst I did not like many of the pots I made there, nor the way in which they were fired, I did learn an awful lot. The potters would sit down and make hundreds of what they were making every day and think nothing of it, certainly not think that they were doing anything special. It shook me to find that instead of making 20 of something in a day, I was

Large terracotta garden pot, made at Wenford Bridge.

Teapot, glazed with Albany slip. Made in America.

expected to make 120 of the same thing—and to find that with practice I could. I enjoyed it and I found it very challenging. Also, I liked the people very much. There were two old men who, when they were younger, used to make between 1500 and 1800 three-inch flower pots each a day, something like two or three every working minute. I am not saying that this is a good thing, just that it is extraordinary, and it does make present day potters look like amateurs. Certainly, I should be far more prepared to listen to men like that than to listen to someone like myself. At 65 they both have an incredible fund of knowledge about throwing and pottery in general. All the pots that I admire, and which I have understood people like Cardew, Leach and many others admire most, were made more often than not in large numbers, not as unique pieces. It's no good sitting down with a Fremington pitcher in front of you and making one, two or three, you will never make them that way. None of us reaches the fluency achieved by the old provincial potters.

Alan Caiger-Smith

Alan Caiger-Smith runs a studio of about seven potters at Aldermaston in Berkshire, producing painted, tin-glazed earthenware, generally for domestic use. He is particularly interested in lustre glaze effects and his research includes a study of methods and techniques used in the past.

When you begin to paint pottery, you have an idea in the back of your mind, which you try to express. After a little while, you find that your brushes will not make certain strokes, or that the idea in your mind does not suit the shape you have chosen. This is really the start of painting pottery rather than painting something else. You discover that your brushes are in a sense like musical instruments; they play in a certain way. As you become more familiar with them, you develop a feeling for what they can do. That is absolutely basic; if you try to use your brush for a movement that is outside its range, the result is a complete mess. I always encourage people who are learning to work out a few brush movements on a piece of newspaper, so that they know roughly what they are going to do—though it is not at all the same as painting on a curved surface. Then, you have to be aware of the curve, knowing that it will extend parts of your strokes to produce a very different effect from the same strokes done on a flat piece of paper. Your sensitivity to the brushes and the shape is something that comes slowly. We have a few pretty simple shapes here which learners will make and paint as an introduction to the repertoire of the brushes.

You have also to remember, in tin-glaze technique, that you are painting on a powdery surface. As the glaze is very absorbent, you cannot make elongated strokes because the brush would run out of colour. There is a certain staccato feel about the painting; you are limited in the length of stroke that you can make, for the powdery glaze soaks up the water so that you need to reload the brush.

Traditional tin-glaze decoration is usually rather careful, meticulous even. Before painting was allowed to start, the pattern was marked out with powdered charcoal pricked through paper pounces. Well, that was one way of doing it, and it could be very effective, but I never really wanted to do that kind of work. All our painting is very much freer, and we often work without any markings on the pot to indicate the arrangement of the pattern. You develop a sense. If you mark out in fives, say, you can space it all out equally without using your eye. On the other hand, if you paint freely, you may make a mess of the first pot, and the second, but you build up enough experience to know where a three, a five, and so on, are going to be. I think, in addition, you can acquire considerable control of the brushwork by working freely.

In some cases, we keep actual examples as a record of shapes and brushwork, but in others we have no pattern worked out before we start painting. The pattern is in somebody's mind—you have a vague idea of what you are going to paint and then you bring it to life. Then, I think, when it really works, you feel that the painting is not premeditated. The pattern takes on a certain vigour, which I do not think it would have if it were always worked out beforehand and then executed on the pot.

The more you go on working, the more you begin to think out the shape and the painting together. Everybody who paints on pottery finds that to take a shape and then think 'How will I decorate that?' usually results in

Interior of lustred bowl, shown in colour on p. 18.

Bird, thrown and hand built, and bowl with relief decoration at rim, both tin-glazed earthenware painted in red lustre.

something pretty uninteresting. As far as possible, you need to have a general conception of how you are going to paint the pot when you are throwing it, so that the two things go together. The term 'decoration', applied to colour or brushwork on pots, suggests something which was put on as an afterthought. I prefer to talk about 'painted pottery', which implies a whole, a pot that is made to be painted, in a shape that was intended for painting. The brushwork has, to some extent, been foreseen before the pot was ever made, and the result is a unity instead of two separate ideas forced together.

To some extent, you are influenced in your choice of pattern by what you have been looking at. Let us say you have been to Turkey or Scandinavia, you are affected by buildings, landscapes, clothes, pictures, and so on, but not in a very literal or obvious way. I have often found it more effective to try to recapture something that I particularly liked than to consult some visual record, such as photographs. The search for a memory that may not be very precise, but is certainly alive, will actually set in motion a lot of other ideas. For example, I painted a bowl with a pattern that arose from the memory of a pomegranate that I ate after supper one night in Portugal. If you slice a pomegranate across, you see extraordinary seed formations, a curiously shaped core and, of course, the orange-red colour. This stuck in my mind, for some reason, and the pattern came not from looking at the fruit, but from the memory of it. The same is true of motifs you may see in a rug, or a building, or another piece of pottery. If you like it, your instinct is to derive from it. In theory, it would be very easy to photograph something you liked and paint from the picture, but you would learn absolutely nothing by it, and the result would be pretty dead.

The form in which some of the painting appears on the pots is not simply a matter of responding to the brushes. If you were inspired solely by what the brush does, you would end up with something pretty vacant. A lot of the painted devices and forms that evolve on our pottery depend a great deal on what is going on in our minds and feelings when we are painting; instead of simply going through a series of fairly decorative motions, the brush expresses something in the back of the painter's mind that he may not be able to put in words. I know that is true, not only of me, but of several other people here. When you are working on a bowl, you develop a feeling about whether the painting is strong and dense or light and gentle, whether it is quiet or full of energy, and so on. In this way, if a pot is really well painted it is not decorated simply to make it agreeable. The painting has to have some sort of coherent meaning, a definite character or mood of its own, which is more than merely a pleasing colour. We all find that we have a conviction, without knowing why, that certain patterns must be painted in

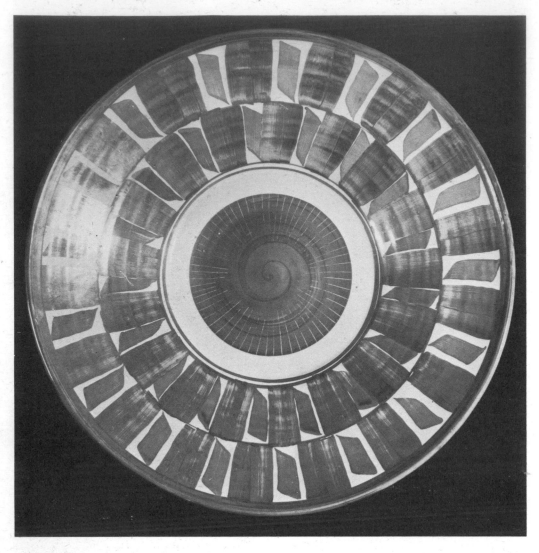

*Large dish with geometrical pattern painted in shades of red and silver lustre;
radiating lines scratched through colour at centre.*

certain colours, or combinations of colour, and not in others. All this is
something to do with the feeling that you have while painting.

Sometimes, brush strokes can be enlivened by scratched decoration. The
colour dries almost immediately when you paint, leaving you with a layer
of powdery glaze coated by a film of pigment through which you can make
scratches. You have to be very careful not to scratch right through to the
clay underneath. I do it with porcupine quills—marvellous things. I was
given some by Michael Cardew. You can also use the end of a brush handle.

*Right. ELIZABETH FRITSCH. Large jar in coiled stoneware with counter-
point pattern painted in slip.*

Bowl, painted resist pattern with blue ground.

We do a certain amount of wax resist with melted wax or an emulsion. It is something especially to do with studio work, almost inapplicable to industrial pottery. I do not usually give it to beginners to do, because you really have to move fast and you cannot correct a mistake. You have to be able to foresee fairly definitely how you are going to work. The technique is not at all traditional. In fact, I do not think it was ever used in early tin-glaze pottery, for very good reasons.

From the point of view of the practitioner, it is better not to think in terms of whether methods are traditional or not. Some which were used in the past can be very relevant, but I would not stick to any technique if I could not make use of it. Wax resist can achieve most beautiful, expressive effects. It is also a very pleasing technique to use. The fact that it was little used for brushwork in the past is incidental.

We use some colours that are never seen in traditional tin-glaze pottery, French, Italian, Dutch, or anything else. The browns come about in wood firings, as they need a certain amount of reduction. All the traditional potteries avoided a reducing atmosphere because it was apt to spoil the glazes. We mix most of our own colours from a basic range of oxides (iron,

Left. DANKA NAPIORKOWSKA & ROGER MICHELL. Lidded jar, thrown and turned, with press moulded details, in lead-glazed earthenware

cobalt, copper, manganese, vanadium, nickel, antimony, chrome, and tin of course). They are all capable of blending with one another, and most of the pigments we use are prepared in the workshop. The small range of colours traditionally used can possibly be explained by the difficulty potters experienced in obtaining any strong colour, partly because the materials were very impure. Strong, pure colours were valued in a way that they are not now that we can come by them so easily. Nowadays, people look for other qualities; they are at least as interested in subtle colours as in the

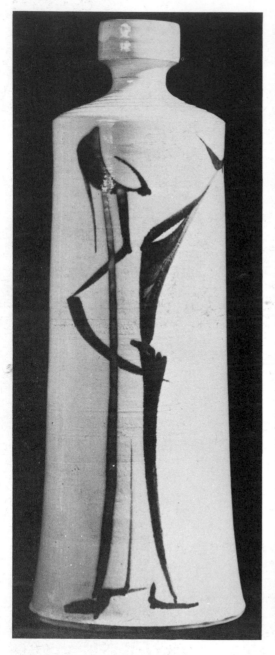

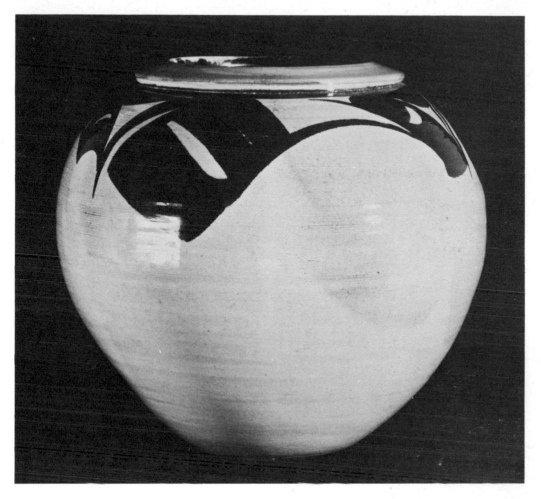

Above: jar with black brushwork at shoulder. Opposite: bottles painted in dark brown, and jug with brushwork in chestnut brown. All thrown in tin-glazed earthenware. Jar and bottles wood fired.

bluest blue or the strongest red. You cannot actually copy an existing shade, say from a fabric, but you can usually find something that will contrast with it, or tone in with it somehow. Of course, it is possible to extend the colour range with the use of enamels, but that would mean a third firing, which increases the cost very considerably.

The lustre was really a natural development from some of my other work. I knew for a long time that I was going to try it, but it was seven or eight years before it was possible to take the risk. A studio workshop has to evolve almost like an industry in reverse. You cannot start off on your own with a wood fired kiln, for instance, because one person cannot make the pots, collect and dry the wood, pack the kiln, stoke it, answer the 'phone and write the necessary letters. If you have two or three people together, then you can use a wood kiln. Most studio potters now start off with a gas or

electric kiln and, if they survive, expand a bit and perhaps then go on to a wood fired kiln.

Our wood kiln is fired about twice a month, four times a year for lustre. Biscuit firings and ordinary glazed, painted work are done there as well. The success rate of lustre is far smaller than that of ordinary firings. In a good lustre firing, we shall probably get out about eighty per cent of the work we put in, in a bad lustre firing we shall maybe get out as little as ten or fifteen per cent, and the rest is mostly waste.

I really had to work more or less blind. English potters are so friendly that if somebody else is using the same technique he will almost certainly give you some advice, but with lustre there was nobody to refer to, and we had to set out with the little I could glean from a few books. We built a special test kiln and had twenty-six firings in it before we got any results at all. So it is something that we have built up practically from nowhere and we are beginning to understand something about it.

I know enough chemistry to have a working understanding of what is going on. The chemistry of ceramics is really very complicated, there's a lot you do not really need to understand completely, but to make pottery without any knowledge of it at all would be extremely unsatisfactory. You would, for one thing, lose a great deal of enjoyment, and you would be

Above: small bowl with blue, black and red brushwork; small lidded bowl and goblet painted in lustre. Opposite: press-moulded plate, approximately 1 ft square, painted with lustre over grey glaze.

unnecessarily at the mercy of the suppliers, whereas if you can do your own tests and make up your own glazes, you will have some comprehension of why you are achieving certain results. You are also better equipped to interpret what goes wrong. If a glaze bubbles and settles again during firing, with a knowledge of chemistry you can probably decide which of the ingredients is causing the white bubbled effect and increase it if you want to, or know how to set about eliminating it.

Worries about the lead in glazes usually arise because journalists do not do their homework. A great many of the best earthenware glazes are made with lead, as are a lot of the best glasses. It is true that a glaze containing lead can be damaging if the proportion of lead and silica is wrongly balanced and if the glaze is seriously underfired. Then, fruit juice or other organic acids kept in the pot will absorb some of the lead from the glaze, and to eat or drink them can be dangerous or even deadly. However, if the glaze is properly compounded, in the sense that the proportion of the ingredients is correct, the release of lead will be minute. All our glazes have by law to be tested in any case. They are properly compounded, they are properly fired, and the lead release is comfortably within the permitted margin—seven parts per million. Our glazes are well within that; one is less than one part per million, and yet it is a lead glaze. You can use lead with total safety, provided you are sensible.

The body of our pots is red, unlike the whitish clays traditionally used abroad. Our clay comes from Fremington in North Devon, where its excellent throwing qualities have been known for centuries. I love throwing, and most of our pots are thrown. One or two forms are press moulded and, from time to time, we make built-up shapes, either with thrown sections, or occasionally coiled or slab built. I think one reason why we do a lot of throwing is that much of our pottery is made for everyday use. The variety of shapes that we try to repeat is something like 120, a ludicrous quantity. If you tried to build them by hand, you could not make them fast enough, and you could not sell them cheaply enough for the sort of useful pottery they are meant to be. And if you cast them, apart from the fact that they would not feel as good, you would end up with thousands of moulds, all requiring storage space and maintenance. That is why no factory I know of makes 120 different shapes—they simply have not room to store the moulds. On the other hand, small workshops using the wheel can produce a really varied range.

I like the feel of thrown pieces, although it's a little bit out of line with modern pottery teaching to use the wheel. It was considered very proper

Bowl with gold and red lustre. Jar painted with animals in chestnut brown.

until about fifteen years ago, but since then the movement has been away from the wheel, which is thought to limit the expressiveness of the shapes that can be made. That is true, as long as you are talking about ceramic sculpture or something like it, but if you are talking about pottery vessels the wheel remains as useful as it ever was and very relevant to any potter who is earning his living by his output. You can, after all, throw fairly quickly. Of course, anyone who is making the same thing all the time becomes extremely fluent, but assistants who are working here will eventually end up with a very wide repertoire of shapes, none of which can be

43

made by rote. All the shapes here have to be made with attention, if they are to be made properly.

On the whole, people here paint what they have made. There is a special reason for that. We do not have Throwers and Painters—everybody does everything. If somebody is learning a shape and fails to get it quite right, he may say, 'Oh it's just Alan's idea, he doesn't like this lovely shape that I've made.' But when he comes to paint it, he will see why the shape should have been a little different. We have a certain shape of bowl which is normally painted on the inside. If it is shaped wrongly, the brushes will not work as they should, and when you come to make the shape again, you will have learnt more about it. This will bring together the shape and the painting. That is the real reason why we all do all the jobs, although it is psychologically good as well.

Shapes which are repeated begin to mature without undergoing any obvious changes. The form evolves by itself, and if you compare two pots made to the same measurement at an interval of about five years you find that the shape has become more agreeable simply by being often made. The same with brush strokes. You may trace back one of your own designs done a few years before, something you have systematically made a dozen times a year, and it has developed, even though you were not trying to change it, or indeed aware of the change as it occurred. I think this secret evolution is an important part of any work which involves repetition. It is a feature of some of the best peasant pottery.

I would say there is a difference between inattentive repetition, which leads eventually to something pretty vacant and facile, and repetition done with attention, which is really a growing thing, giving rise to the process of maturing that you only see long afterwards. Very often, people talk about repetition as if it meant doing exactly the same thing again and again; it really means going through the same kinds of motion repeatedly, without doing precisely the same thing. It struck me particularly because I was so bad to begin with that there was plenty of room for improvement, but it is something that happens even with really skilled people. There is a case for non-repeat work, too, and that has its own reasoning and philosophy. There is simply something about repetition which a lot of people underestimate.

When you do come to break new ground, it can be for a number of reasons. Once, after being ill, I was unable to throw pots on the wheel and took the opportunity to work on a large tile panel with figures in relief. Also, the pottery is open to the public, and the contact is interesting when people ask for things they want and cannot find elsewhere. It is a good challenge, because if an idea is my own, I have probably seen the pot in my mind's eye, and it will turn out to be a version of something I have made before, very likely, whereas if I am asked for a pot that is going to serve a particular purpose, I have to think whether it can be done. Sometimes requests from the public put us under a little pressure—people may ask for painted plates, when we know very well that certain kinds of painting are likely to get confused with sausages, gravy or bacon, and people might try to get their forks into the brush strokes. Nevertheless, it makes for a good relationship with people to know that what you are working on is going to be wanted by someone.

It is sometimes assumed that there is an opposition between craft and industry. This stems, I think, from the entirely different associations they have in people's minds. It is impossible to separate industrialism and craftsmanship. Many features of modern factories already existed in the sixteenth

Dinner plate, one of a set, painted in brownish black.

century. You had there embryonic industrial techniques which were used in small workshops, but were nonetheless extraordinarily close in principle to some of the techniques you will see in use in a big factory today.

I think it is another of those apparent oppositions. Like traditional and non-traditional, industrial and non-industrial are not very helpful categories to consider. In industry, a great deal of craftsmanship is concerned not with the making of the product, but in the handling and maintenance of machines. Craftsmanship is still there, but it has been transferred. If you think of a machine which is going to make plates or dip them, well, that machine has to be made by craftsmen, and it has to be serviced by craftsmen who understand it. I find it sad, in a way, that industry places its craftsmen largely in the maintenance section.

A modern pottery factory does use a small number of craftsmen in production. Some have more throwers than many people would believe, and anybody who is concerned with pattern making is certainly a craftsman working directly on the material. But it is a pity that more modern factories do not take the risk of employing a larger number of people who are working directly in production. They would not lose by it. Denby, for instance, employ nineteen throwers, or they did when I visited them, perhaps there are more now, and about thirty painters painting by hand—not many people realize that. And Denby is one of the most successful English factories, so that there is not an absolute opposition between craftsmanship and industry. I think the difficulty occurs when the factory grows very big, but I would say that for a medium-sized factory, the scope for using hand work is still fairly extensive.

If a factory offered to make my pottery designs, I would be delighted. You see, a small pottery like this is embarrassed by its best sellers, and there are some things that sell so well that we could go on making them all the year round without exhausting the demand. All eight of us could spend the whole time making ovenware and nothing else—so what do you do with your best sellers? You get letters from shops ordering so many of this, that and the other, and in order to protect yourself you say that you are sorry, but you are unable to supply that particular kind of casserole. What you mean is that you are not going to make any more of them because there are other things that you want to make, too. A small pottery can get out of balance in this way, and it seems to me that it would be desirable from both logical and commercial points of view to enter into some contract with a larger producer, who would say, 'You have something you can't make enough of, I have surplus space where I could increase my range. Let me make some of these things, and perhaps pay you a small royalty.' In theory, it sounds absolutely logical and easy, but in practice it is very difficult to find a larger producer who is willing and sufficiently adaptable. If you found such a firm, it would mean that a small workshop could go on being itself without feeling silly and inadequate when it had to stop making things in the quantity that people ask for.

Michael Cardew

Michael Cardew was Bernard Leach's first pupil and he has been making pottery for over fifty years. Influenced by English slipware and also by the native pottery of West Africa, where he worked for many years, he produces wood fired stoneware made to a high standard of craftsmanship for everyday use.

My father was at the Board of Education, as it was called in those days. He was very sympathetic, not at all upset by my being a potter. He was always a collector of things and it was he who used to take the whole family over to Fremington Pottery in North Devon. I used to stand and watch Mr Fishley throw pots. My wheel is like his, made in the same part of the world. I never worked with old Mr Fishley, because I was only a small boy, perhaps not quite ten, when he died in 1911, and I can't really remember him. None of his sons would be a potter, because they could see it was, as a grandson expressed it, a dying industry. That sounds funny now, but it was true in those days. He had one grandson, William Fishley Holland, who was keen and became a very successful potter. He was in North Devon when I was trying to learn to pot and it was he who gave me the first lessons in throwing, if only for about two weeks. Then, I went on teaching myself on my own. I used to be allowed to go into a little pottery in Braunton in the evenings. In spite of trouble with the university for spending my holidays doing the

Four mugs made at St Ives in lead-glazed earthenware with sgraffito inscriptions.

wrong thing, I went on practising throwing until I was free to start as a potter.

I did not know where to go, but I had seen a small paragraph in the Pottery Gazette or one of the trade magazines, saying that an English artist had come back from Japan and had brought a Japanese potter with him. I went down to St Ives and found the Leach pottery in its infancy in 1923. I had not heard of Bernard Leach—very few had—there was just this mention in the paper. I did not pay much attention to the paragraph, but I thought it was worth looking at. I went to the pottery in Truro, which was flourishing in those days, and then to St Ives. Mr Leach was not there, but I was introduced to Shoji Hamada, who was living at the pottery. I did not arrive until it was almost dark—it was early in January—and I asked Hamada whether there was any chance of working there. Hamada said he did not know, but he was leaving England at the end of 1923 and thought perhaps a helper would be needed. So he took me round to see Mr Leach. We walked about two miles by the lanes across the hill in the dark, and then I met Mr Leach for the first time.

Left: earthenware dish with slip trailed decoration inspired by Persian original.
Above: stoneware dish with sgraffito decoration.

I think the reason why I was taken on at the Leach pottery was that I was madly keen about the English slipware tradition. People think Leach was interested only in oriental stoneware, but that is not so. He was the man who started the slipware revival. My origin in pottery had been the traditional earthenware with slip decoration that had been going on in North Devon for about three hundred years. There is none left in this country, but it was exported by the shipload to Baltimore in the second half of the seventeenth century. This lovely yellow lead-glazed slipware was out of fashion in England, I suppose, because of the coloured delftware already being made at that time, but it was considered good enough for the colonies. It was quite light, chipped probably. All the remaining pieces are broken and reconstructed. In the eighteenth century, the colonists stopped wanting slipware as they were making their own pots, and the Devon potters began to concentrate on country ware. Their only artistic work was the very fancy harvest jugs with rhymes on the front; old Mr Fishley carried on some of that tradition. I like them less now, but I used to adore them.

I suppose Leach thought he could use this enthusiast, and when I left the university, I went straight to the St Ives pottery. It was very hard work, and a very hard life really, in those days, because it was only beginning, and hand to mouth all the time. Bernard was selling locally and having shows. He had an exhibition in Japan, which I think he lived on.

What aroused the interest of people in England is, I suppose, a pretty long story. After all, it's more than fifty years. Just persistence on Leach's part. It is difficult now to imagine the Victorian and Edwardian standards of what art pottery ought to be like. Terrible stuff—it was generally brightly coloured, extremely well finished and very, very overworked, with meticulous craftsmanship and all that sort of thing. People could not recognize any of these desiderata in the work that came out of the Leach pottery, because it looked to them like pieces of mud. They couldn't make head or tail of it at all. Bernard used to send work to the Artificers' Guild, a shop in Conduit Street where they sold Victorian arts and crafts. I went there in about 1922. I had not been to the Leach pottery by that time, but I had heard about

Dish, press-moulded in stoneware; Vumé lily design painted in blue.

Stoneware teapot, jug and bottle, pattern of horizontal bands, partly smoothed by finger.

the shop and I went to see what was there. They had little pots and things that I could not understand either, because of course I did not know much about oriental pottery.

The Devonshire slipware had sgraffito decoration like the very early European, Byzantine earthenware. It is essentially a southern technique. All the kinds of slipware that Mr Leach was keen on reviving said rather less to me, although I have grown to like them. The trailed slip feathering is a northern tradition, mainly from Staffordshire and Derbyshire. It's a maddening job—it's a question of the weight you put on. The danger is that if you do not use enough weight your hand trembles, but if you do it too firmly you get a long pull that drags rather. The subtlety of a slight pull is far more beautiful. If I were to do it, which I don't now, I would use one of those wonderful porcupine whiskers. The African porcupine is a much bigger animal than the American version, with much longer quills— absolutely lethal. For the painting I do now, I use a Japanese brush and black pigment. That tradition is, above all, oriental and also Mediterranean.

All my time at Winchcombe, when I made what some people suppose are my best pots, I used only earthenware. People had started coming to the pottery, even in those days, to buy pots. We sold seconds and so on, and once or twice I sent work to joint exhibitions. The National Society of Painters, Sculptors, Engravers and Potters provided the first chance for potters to be admitted to the society of the elect. I exhibited there—that was when I became known. Leon Underwood, the sculptor, was there, too. This man, whom I had never met before, came up to me as I was unpacking and

asked 'Who made these wonderful things?' I looked at him very blankly and said 'Which wonderful things?' Then he went and told all his friends, who bought pots, Charles Cundall, Frank Dobson . . . As a result, I sold everything to fellow exhibitors. But Charles Marriott, then art critic of *The Times*, came and gave the show a very good write-up, and I joined the society of Staite Murray and Bernard Leach.

An architect, Sidney Greenslade, who was a great collector of pots, bought a good deal of my stuff, although he had done most of his buying by that time. He had collected Martinware and it was he who introduced me to one of the Martin brothers. They were not very impressed and nor was I. I knew what I wanted to do, and I knew it would not be like their work. People were tremendously keen on them, but I did not really like what they had done—I still don't. So much was influenced by the pre-Raphaelites—pots with things growing all over them.

The modern potter I admire most is Hamada, although I do not really understand Japanese pottery. Nevertheless, everything Hamada does is tremendously genuine. The principle is, I am sure, that it's clay. It looks like something made out of clay and it looks 'kind', Hamada's favourite word. He requires of the body of his pot that it be healthy and, of the pot itself, that it be kind. Even photographs of his pots show a sort of warmth in the material. As one of the tests of pottery, it is very esoteric. You see the quality in most of Bernard Leach's work, and the Leach Pottery regular products.

The clay sits there and it glows. The treatment is right. No violence has been done to the material. Nature and natural materials are used in a more or less natural or harmonious way, and nothing artificial is imposed on them. This applies to nearly all oriental pottery, except the very last stuff made for Europeans, or the most ornate things. The traditional oriental approach is to treat nature in a tactful manner, not to try and force it, because nature is your friend and your enemy. You have to make it produce what you want, you cannot just let it go, but the modern western attitude is that you clamp down on it. A persuasive treatment of nature is what I admire in pots—that's what I like about Hamada, especially his early work. As with all good pots, you have to get to know them. Pots are like people, and you cannot tell for certain whether a pot is really going to be a friend until you get to know it. That is why it seems to me so important to use the things in one's everyday life.

Stoneware plate with incised inscription to commemorate christening of Michael Cardew's grandson, and (left) vase and jar in stoneware.

Michael Casson

Michael Casson was responsible with Victor Margrie for setting up a course at Harrow School of Art intended to train professional potters. He now works as a full-time potter making domestic stoneware and some porcelain in the workshop which he shares with his wife Sheila in Great Missenden, Buckinghamshire.

Like many people, I stumbled into pottery. At first, I was a painter in a minor way. After the war, I went to an Emergency Training College, really to become a teacher, but also to learn more about painting. The course then required you to take up a craft as well—a chap came round with a list of crafts for students to choose from. That was in 1946. I did some teaching and then went back to do painting at Hornsey School of Art, but changed to pottery at the beginning of the course. Hornsey was little help at that time to anyone who wanted to be a potter and earn a living at it. Afterwards my wife, Sheila, and I gradually went through the process of teaching ourselves the basics. It takes a long time to learn that way. You can only take some short cuts if you have a good teacher.

Although I enjoyed my Art School experience, I felt that it was the wrong way to go about educating someone who wanted to make a living at a craft. Certain elements, like painting and drawing, were very valuable—they made you look and see. But down-to-earth practical help was lacking, and discipline, too—the self-discipline needed to learn a craft. So when Victor Margrie and I started the Harrow course in 1963, these were the thoughts in my mind. Victor looked back, I know, with kinder memories of Art School, and it was he who always stressed those aspects of the course that would sow the seed of further, broader development that he hoped would flower later on. I certainly agreed with this attitude and, in fact, I have always believed that the two 'poles' of ceramics, pottery as fine art and pottery as functional ware, merge so imperceptibly into one another that I do not make a distinction between most kinds; there is simply good work and not so good work, or work that interests me and work that does not.

Harrow was a collaboration between staff and students. We were conscious that there was a growing demand for functional pots. I was dividing my time between teaching and my own work as a professional potter, and we knew that the demand was building up rapidly. We felt, too, that no other art school had that in mind. In fact, most of them were trying to go in headlong retreat from throwing. I think one of Harrow's main achievements was to help to bring back throwing again. We just provided a

Bowl in stoneware. Pots in porcelain, blue celadon glaze.

course that aimed to fill the gap. Colin Pearson came in as the third member of the team and, from then on we welcomed such people as Bernard Leach and Harry Davis, and others like Hans Coper, who would come to give us a talk or simply be there with the students. It was a tremendous experience and worked marvellously for me for about ten years. That was about the right length of time; I needed then to get back to my own work. I had been giving as much as I knew, but we were all receiving a lot back. We had first rate students.

While I was there, about 110 people completed the two year course. Many of them have since set up as professional potters; nearly all are still connected with pottery in some way. We tried to select students with the idea that they should be strongly motivated. They were mainly in their mid twenties and many were highly qualified in other disciplines. They had to be confident enough to take criticism and use it, which was very important.

Working potters do risk becoming complacent, of course. Who else in Britain can claim to sell everything they make? There is a definite need for people to be discriminating and possibly to say 'What a rotten mug! How dare you put it on the market?' I do concern myself with quality, but I also sympathize with the people for whom the work mainly means an attractive way of life. I only hope they can combine that feeling with a concern for high standards and produce good ceramics.

It is hard to define why people buy our pots and enable us to live this stimulating life. I recently attended a series of lectures on art and archeology. The archeologists, who dominated the course, were talking about computers and, in fact we hardly saw any archeological artefacts the whole time. Towards the end, however, an old Greek professor got up holding an African figure and declared. 'This has resonance, I can feel it. I know this is genuine!' He got a great reception because for the first time, although it was emotional and highly subjective, he was talking about something we instantly understood without recourse to mathematics or statistics. I feel this resonance has something to do with the appeal of pots. I know also that a lot of it arises from the difference between studio pottery and mass produced ware. I am not saying that studio work is better, because I believe that some industrial pottery is very fine indeed, but there is always a certain type of person whose whole life style prompts him to search for something out of the ordinary. This is not necessarily the best motive, but it may combine with selection for resonance, or appreciation of the subtleties of form and colour. The hand potter does not clear away what his hand and the materials impart, whereas industry is not associated with the hand so much as with machines.

One of the attractions of pottery as a way of life is definitely the challenge. I think I am at an age now when one should not get too comfortable. It is very important for me to try to drive myself on, not competitively or for financial gain, but in the work itself. I still have ideas to develop that stem from 25 years ago or more, when I started. At present, I am trying to fuse

Stoneware storage jar with dry ash glaze.

inlaid decoration in porcelain to a clay that is almost high fired earthenware, with the idea of making tiles and wall plaques. The technique resembles the making of so-called encaustic tiles. I might also try this idea out on pots as well.

There are many things that I cannot yet do, many things that I have to experiment with—the technical aspects of porcelain, for example, a bigger range of glazes, more knowledge of clay bodies. If our wood kiln goes well, I shall want to build a bigger one some day, and then there are other fuels of which I have little experience. I have seen a lot of fire at second hand through people like Walter Keeler, who was with us at Harrow (and is there still); we fired every conceivable kind of kiln from sawdust, bonfire, right through to saltglaze. I encouraged it and saw it all going on, but

basically I am not a good engineer and kilns are, in a way, machines. I have learned a lot from other people which I am willing to pass on. I think I can translate and explain, but I do not have the fund of detailed knowledge possessed by, say, Colin Pearson. The painterly side of me is not usually the kind of source from which you would expect a technical person to arise.

Time is a very important element in my manner of working. In the main, I like speedy methods because they suit me, temperamentally. For the most part, I dip pots in coloured slip and decorate them with my thumb, my nail, or a piece of porcupine quill that Michael Cardew gave me a long time ago. I am not a meticulous person—the inlaid tile technique is as painstaking as I am going to get (as far as I can see now). I have found that a slower kind of care does not usually work for me—the end product lacks satisfaction and, in the end, I like swiftness. With the inlaid porcelain, the decoration itself is fairly fast. The slower work comes in cleaning the surface afterwards, but that is just a mechanical process.

Though I also like small, delicate things, when I see a lot of big pots around I feel happy. I find bigware very exciting: there is something very

Stoneware bowl with inlaid decoration under transparent glaze. Opposite: dish, glaze flecked with iron; jars with dry ash glaze, glazed porcelain lids.

Porcelain bowl with sgraffito decoration.   Opposite: stoneware bowl with inlaid porcelain decoration.

physical about it. At Harrow, some of the students caught us up frighteningly fast in throwing, and even in throwing big pots some would overtake us. I remember a chap called Dave Drury throwing 37 pounds of clay on a kick wheel. I could not even turn it round satisfactorily, but then he was twenty years younger than I was. The traditional way of throwing really large pots is the method Svend Bayer uses. He adds coils of clay on top of the base he has thrown and then throws the coil up. Historically they were never thrown in one piece. Few of our generation can touch the traditional throwers. With so much more technology to complicate things, we risk learning a little about all sorts of aspects instead of going very deeply into one particular method.

I want to go on mainly with throwing. I cannot see myself doing any hand building now, except maybe the tiles I spoke of. But then, in years to come, I may be forced by circumstances to make pots by other ways. If that happened I should be happy to go back to painting and, certainly, hand building, perhaps coiling. There are so many superb ways of making pots, but while I can I shall keep throwing. Making is a fine way of living and, I find, very satisfying, very fulfilling, physically, emotionally and intellectually. 'The hands make the head clever,' Michael Cardew said.

Storage jar, dark glaze on lid and rim; large jug in stoneware with brushed decoration.

Elizabeth Fritsch

Elizabeth Fritsch now lives at Digswell House Arts Trust. She creates unique coiled stoneware pots which she paints with coloured slips in geometrical, sometimes illusionistic, patterns.

Each of my pots is formed and then painted by hand; it is meant to be held and touched as well as seen. Thus, for a museum to shut pottery in glass cases is like asking 'Please do not look' at an exhibition of paintings.

I see pottery as hand held architecture on a very human scale that is half way between seashells, which I love partly for their amazing colours, and man-made houses, where it is possible for the physical function of being a house to be partly symbolic, as in the case of cathedrals or temples. Similarly with my pottery, each piece is a humble pot and at the same time a kind of metaphor. The fact that the forms are always vessels (as opposed to any other kind of sculpture) makes the act of containing intrinsic to the work.

Front and back of bottle and (opposite) oval bowl. All coiled stoneware, painted in slip.

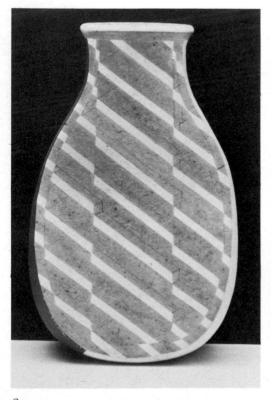 

The contents may be life-giving food or drink, whose ephemeral nature, like that of flowers, makes a happy contrast with the strong, lasting qualities of the vessel. On the other hand, the contents might be accidental or unexpected or surrealistic—sand, pebbles, mirrors or odd bits of human clutter. Or, again, the vessel may enclose the freedom of sheer, empty space. W. B. Yeats's image of 'the basin of the mind', with its connotations of receiving, holding, mixing and pouring out, can be regarded as symbolic of creative activity.

The idea of a pot's total function is thus built up from the physical, utilitarian and homely elements of kitchen with the spiritual, artistic and exciting components of temple. A pot is essentially rooted in the ordinary. My task is to transmit through the ordinary some measure of magic. To have been moved by the aura of a particular place or person or work—a piece of music perhaps—and then to have to try (to some extent hopelessly, knowing unavoidable limitations) to communicate such a mood via the clay is where the basic inspiration springs for me. The mystery of such moods emanates through the subconscious, so I do not apply intellectual thoughts when I am working. In fact, I often work with the television on, or with music playing, because I find it helpful not to have my consciousness focussed on the work. Hopefully, the subconscious can emerge. Similarly, formal control of the clay itself and a rigorous, almost acrobatic approach to technique are helpful only when they have reached a fluency over the years which frees mind and material to act effortlessly and spontaneously.

ELIZABETH FRITSCH

Cup and flask in coiled stoneware; illusionistic designs painted in coloured slips.

Elemental relationships are fundamental to the work, for example the earthbound clay aspires to become airborne in the dynamics of the form, in the harmonies of colour, and in the shifts between two and three dimensions. Water is evoked sometimes by colour and particularly by the rims, which reflect the moods of still or flowing water. Fire, which transforms the body in the kiln, also affects the colours, sometimes in an unpredictable way.

I should like to make pots for use in the kitchen in thick, heavy-duty porcelain, possibly to be slip cast, to make everyday pots as well as aspirational, airborne looking ones. But there is some instinct that does not easily allow me to make utilitarian ware. I do not plan pieces in advance, so when my hands are actually shaping the clay I find myself turning each piece into something different—a new experiment—which has more to do with making an art object. It may be the amount of time I squander on a piece of work, even when I may not want to, or when the time from a practical point of view is not really there to spend.

My work is tending to become more illusionistic—for example in the shifting like a shadow between two and three dimensions. I am also moving more towards the idea of groups where the relationship between the pots is more alive than the pots individually. I like the fact that their inter-relationships are insubstantial. I should like to get as far away from substance as I possibly could, but in an energetic way, without becoming spineless. The

painting I put on is always moving towards making the pots more airborne and dynamic. William Blake is a painter whose work I love, and I am very attracted to the movement he achieves away from substance towards the energetic and airborne. But paradoxically I also like the fact of pots' being tactile, actually there and earthborne in the hands.

Seeing and touching relate to various aspects of the form and surface of the pots. The shape of the foot is pretty arbitrarily chosen at the start. I simply let a shape emerge which follows logically the pattern the foot has determined. Normally, the base is rounded, without any protruding foot ring, because I like the form to rest as comfortably and completely as possible in the palms of the hands. And in the standing pot I seek the dynamic, airborne appearance of a rounded, uninterrupted base. When the shape has built up, I have to make what may be my first really conscious decision, of how to finish it off. The rim, which is the culminating point of the vessel, determines its whole dynamic. It embodies the mystical division between inside and outside, as well as being the focus of the action in drinking or pouring. I tend to emphasize the rim by doubling or trebling the thickness of the clay, or else by trying to reduce it to Donne's 'airey thinnesse'.

On the surface, I try to approach a natural mattness, freshness and softness (such as that of, say, wood, silk or skin) which contrasts with the hard resonance of stoneware. The texture must respond to the touch of fingertips in the same way that the form responds to the whole hands.

ELIZABETH FRITSCH

Colour (fragmented light) used as a force aspires to elevate. It is elemental in essence; painted and then transformed in the fire, it can be airy as well as earthy. The contrast between these elements provides the opportunity for play and emphasis in relationship to form. My idea has always been to make use of the hallucinatory powers of colour, to achieve an atmosphere that makes the mind wander. Piero della Francesca did with colour what I should like to be able to do one day. He used earth colours, as one does very often in ceramics, with matt effects brilliantly spaced.

Pattern, when married to colour and form, works in a way that is directly analogous to rhythm in music and dance; Jerzy Grotowski said in *Towards a Poor Theatre*, 'A man in an elevated spiritual state uses rhythmically articulated signs i.e. begins to dance and sing.' Through the patterning on pots, I try to catch a glimpse of underlying and overlapping structures using systematic methods, like counterpoint, but I like the dance of colour

and form to be as unselfconscious and accessible as it undoubtedly is in folk art and music all over the world. I like to use precisely articulated geometrical patterns and contrive optical games, without, I hope, losing the feeling as it were of improvising on a given form which is the blank pot. Flat, angular patterns play off rounded forms in the same way as the illusion of full, round dimensions in pots which, on inspection, turn out to be drastically flattened, and belong to what I regard as a 2½ dimensional tactile and optical adventure.

Music is an important source of inspiration for me. I love the metaphysical implications of its capacity to transfer exultation. I try to measure space with the same precision and freedom used in measuring musical time. I like to conjure up visual equivalents of musical patterns, such as *arpeggio,* counter-

Coiled stoneware pot painted in coloured slips. Opposite: optical Moon Pocket.

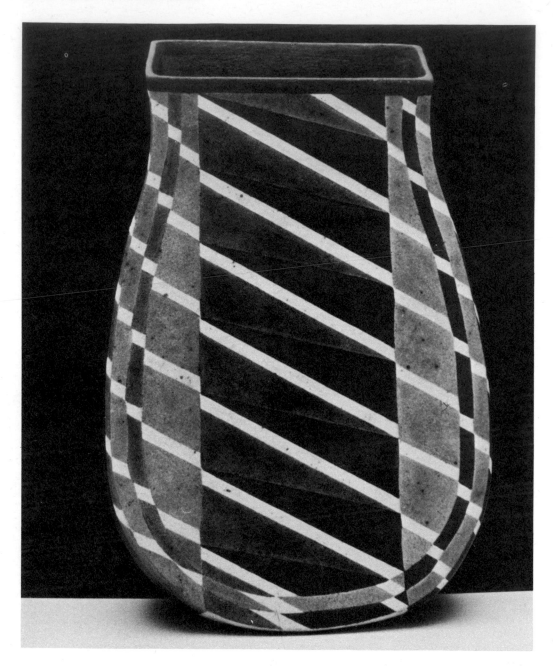

point, cross rhythms, and so on—again my aim of transcending substance.

With any luck, the time I spend in making and painting achieves a quality of timelessness in the work, though I do not want to make ethnic or backward-looking pottery, in spite of having made some early on, for there are aspects of the machine age that I love, especially those which might one day be in accord with 'man as the aim of production' as opposed to 'production being the aim of man' (Karl Marx). I could not work without wanting some distinctively twentieth century moods to come through.

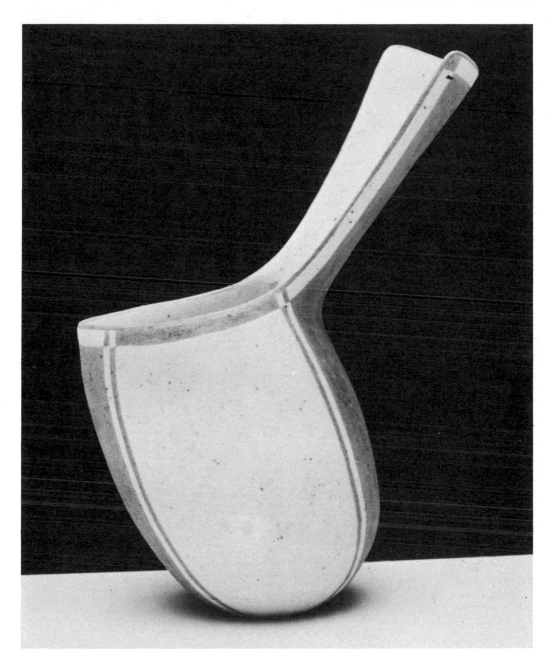

Coiled stoneware pot painted in coloured slip. Opposite: jar, flat in section.

I should still make pots, even if I did not have to sell them for a living. I make them primarily as love tokens to give, not as commodities to sell. This means that each piece is different from all others, and in a romantic sense, I imagine that money does not buy them even when they have been sold. I am simply thankful to be able to make a living out of work which I enjoy doing.

Ian Godfrey

Ian Godfrey shares a studio in London. He produces pottery based on functional shapes; often a thrown base is decorated with applied motifs taken from ancient Eastern ceramics and metalwork, or pierced designs, carved in stoneware. Some of his pots contain hidden landscapes or animal figures.

I had first made pots when I was eight, and did pottery one day a week when I started as a student at Camberwell Art School, around 1957. That's when I met Lucie Rie, who was teaching there. I have known Lucie since I was seventeen. She always claims that she did not teach me anything, but she did, by her mere presence. One thing that she said she did not think ethical was the use of a penknife, which is my main tool. All my work is carved when it is practically dry. At the time, people said, 'This tool is for one job and that's for another. There are certain things you do and some you don't.' I do not feel that.

I started on the pierced bowls almost as exercises, like playing scales. I cut into the edge of a bowl to see how much piercing it will take and what

Village bowl thrown and carved in stoneware. Opposite: small pierced plate, thrown and carved in porcelain.

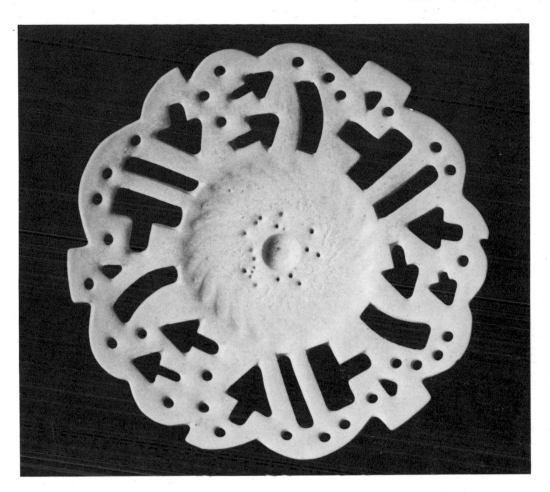

sort of design I can produce on the broad rim, taking it to extremes without causing the pot to split. When high fired the bowls are surprisingly strong. I use a mixture of red earthenware with St Thomas's clay (a high temperature grey stoneware containing a lot of sand) and a very rough brick making clay with a high content of particles that are already fired. The three clays combined, one very smooth, one semi-smooth, and one very high firing and rough, provide a good texture for carving with my penknife, while the fragments of fired clay enable me to fire thick pots without losing a high proportion through splitting in the kiln. I like to use glazes which achieve the effects found on rocks, lichen and earthy tints, very little added colour in fact.

After working on my own for three or four years, I just had my basement workshop in the City Road and hundreds of pots. I wanted to continue working in the same kind of way that I had at art school, not to become concerned with whether I could sell my pots. A few people were interested, enough to keep things going. I used to deliver pots on a bicycle with a rucksack on my back, and still do, but now people come to me as well, which is very inspiring.

I first started exhibiting at Primavera in 1962—years ago. I was sharing a workshop with two or three other potters. We had a kiln on tick from the bank and one wheel, which we built, based on an old, primitive, Egyptian or Arabic style that you simply kick round with your foot. I mainly did slab work, very crudely made and rather fierce.

My chief interest had been painting, indeed I am still very interested and will continue to be. In the past, it was rather pushed aside, but even then I used occasionally to draw on the floor with water on a Japanese brush when everyone had left the workshop at night. (The floor provides a wonderful surface when it has clay on it, and the drawing simply disappears.) I was forced to specialize in pottery, which I did not like to do. The CAC bursary has helped me to get back to observing life outside the confines of a workshop through painting.

I developed an awareness of sculpture through a marvellous Czech, Karl Vogel, who made his students work in a very figurative way. He used to play chamber music, usually Smetana, Dvorak, Janacek, and so on, to his class, and I became fascinated by the relationship between music and the other arts. I am still making musical pots, really. All the elements are ones that might have influenced composers of the romantic age, birds, flowers, little temples . . .

I am extremely inspired by antiquities. I used to go to museums when I was very young. At about twelve, I collected Greek terracottas, when they were very cheap. I always used to be taking days off school to go to the British Museum and look at lovely objects. Later I used to want, but could not afford, what I saw there—Chinese bronzes, for instance—and I often rushed down to the pottery to try to recapture some of the essence of things I had seen, very consciously maintaining the study elements of the work, rather than consider the commercial side. I still spend a proportion of what I get for the sale of my pots on things that please me and will provide some inspiration to feed back into future pots.

My favourite pots of all are some fifth-century Korean bowls with cut out decoration, beautifully inspired by metal forms, always in grey coloured clay before they discovered glazes. Another of my favourites was made by Koreans who were forced into Japan by the dictator Hideoshi in the sixteenth century. They were the ones who inspired the Japanese to do their staggering brushwork, so rarely done properly now. I think Bernard Leach managed it—I have a tile of his that dates from the 1920s. There's a beautiful brown hanging pot by Shoji Hamada, probably a water pourer used in the tea ceremony. It is beaten and has a very rough foot, marvellously spontaneous when Hamada does it, though I would not dare to copy it.

I like metalware. The ritualistic spoons, again Korean, from the Silla dynasty (57 BC–AD 736) are almost too beautiful to look at. I have a ninth-

Village casket, birds inside. Pilgrim bottles with mountain village, and (right) after tenth-century Chinese original.

IAN GODFREY

century Korean bronze bowl, like one in the Victoria & Albert Museum, completely plain. The feeling that I get from the items in my collection I try to bring into my work and in a crude way I do try to carve in the same spirit.

Sometimes I haven't the self-discipline to overcome my disinclination to get down to work. I sit about for hours without really doing anything, and then suddenly work furiously into the night. But I do not believe in waiting for inspiration. I believe in making things constantly.

I never throw anything away, I simply adapt it. If pots break, I mend them, and if they break in an interesting way, I make it look intentional, which may in turn lead me on to a new conception. I often used to find that round bowls warped out of shape. I find it rather interesting, so that I devised a method of making what a psychiatrist friend who collects them calls 'anxiety bowls'. They certainly are nerve-racking objects to make, I thought I might as well make a feature of the distortion by adding a handle and a flower, which would balance each other across the very tiny base, and turn it into something that was deliberately warped.

Apart from the fact that it is complete agony some of the time, the making of pots is a wonderful way of being employed. I see it as living in a sort of fantasy world, but I am employed by my customers and clients, or whatever you like to call them, the people who love pots, to go on making them.

Landscape with village and boat. Opposite: bridges in green stoneware and teapot.

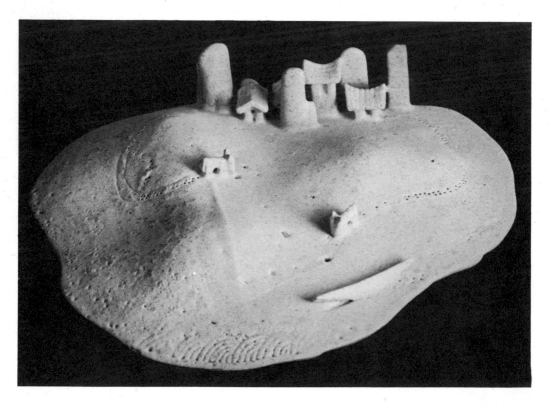

 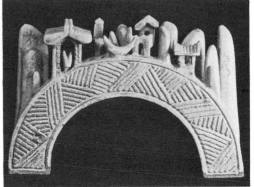

Barrel pilgrim bottles with rainbow handle, and (right) animals.

There are enough people around who are sympathetic, now. I always had practical problems in running a workshop, but I am now able, not to expand exactly—I would never want to do that—but to live. In fact, I would like a smaller workshop with perhaps one other person. I would always want to share, either with a student just learning, or anybody who was compatible to work with, because I like to have other people about. I thrive on an exchange of ideas.

I often think it would be valuable to take time off abroad, doing something completely different, and come back to a small London workshop with enough extra stimulus and information to work harder on ideas, planning and working from the influence of another environment, and producing much more slowly. I have a great desire to cut down on the number of pieces I produce and simply explore one theme, for instance. I find present pressures place me in danger of turning out work in large quantities, I think in rather a stereotyped way. I have been very bored by working for

some of my later exhibitions because I was making all these safe pots. There was very little excitement. On the other hand, it is only exhibitions that save one from extinction as an individual potter.

Economically, you cannot raise your prices dramatically, and I would not wish to, but you can create a rarity in what you do, working out ideas that much more surely and calmly, without having to rush things through. I am sometimes asked to produce groups of pieces, ten or twenty miniature teapots, something like that, although I only started making miniature teapots almost as models for larger ones, exercises in the same way as the pierced bowls. I feel a resistance to this because in making pots for immediate sale you lose the opportunity to have groups of them around to study and evaluate, and you lose the time you need to decide what may be right or wrong with a particular form. Learning from the pots you make helps you to overcome the problems of setting out. Now that I have worked for fifteen years as a potter, I feel that the future can hold good in many more, different directions. Ultimately, I would like my work to retain its freshness, spontaneity and delight for me and, hopefully, for other people.

Mo Jupp

Mo Jupp teaches at Harrow and Farnham Art Schools. His own work comprises individual pieces made by a variety of methods: sometimes slab-built, thrown and cut, press-moulded or slip cast. To his clay forms he has applied decoration of feathers, wire and other materials.

The continual argument over whether certain things are art or not is not very relevant—if you think it's art, it is art. All the things I make are to do with how I feel, not how I drink. I have something I want to produce, and it is concerned with an emotion, but there is a craft attached to it, like the sort of skill that was involved in painting in the days when you needed to know how to grind colour for yourself. I find that pottery students, who have to spend a week or two of the term in another department to broaden their outlook, will take quite readily to painting or rug making, while Fine Art students who come into the pottery department will have ideas for something they want to make, but they just do not know how to set about making it. Once they have learned the craft, some people will stay crafts-

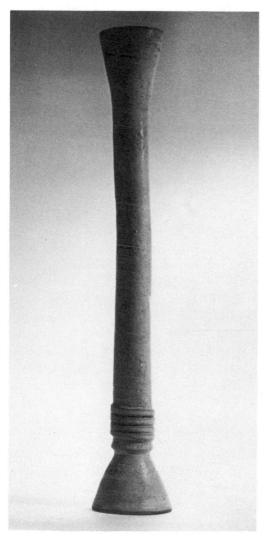
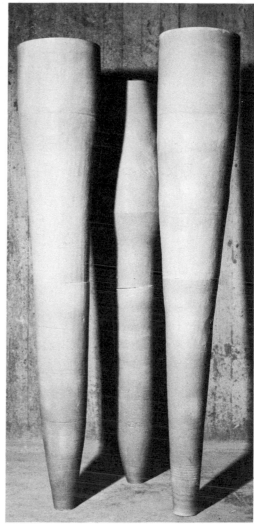

Temple for Woman, porcelain, celadon glaze. White glazed pots, thrown.

men, in that they will work from illustrations, they will convert, say photographs into line drawings. Other people will manage to create some vitality.

The thing about pottery is that the technique is very simple. It is what you make and how you do it that decide its importance. The qualities really come down to volume– a pot is rather like an egg, with an inner reservoir of energy separated from the outside by a thin shell. What is contained is not a vacuum, but a volume trying to get out. Everyone I know has managed to achieve this sometimes; I do it maybe once in every ninety pots, and Hans Coper is the only one who brings it off every time.

In this country, we put everything we have on the walls and all flat surfaces. The Japanese do not do that; they keep their collections in a separate place and bring out one or two pieces at a time. When they have seen enough of them they put them away and bring out another two. That appeals to me. As an artist, you tend to isolate things. I do not look at things I do not want to see.

In the same way, I do not feel that I look at, say, trees in the way that a painter might look at them. I see a silhouette, but I ignore the trunk until branches actually come off it and I may concentrate on the way they join. Women's legs, too, are pleasing, but some are beautiful in a pottery way. I once had a clay pipe that had some of the characteristics of knees in the join of the stem to the bowl. I have often tried to achieve that in pots without yet being able to—at present I cannot see a way of doing it.

When you become involved in anything, there are some areas you are switched on to, but the back of your mind is always half aware, collecting, because you are never sure when you are going to see something that will be useful. I try to impress on students when they start that they have spent nearly twenty years picking up information of which they are unaware, because they use teapots, go places with their parents, and so on. When they go to art school, it's like opening a flood gate, everything flows out, leaving nothing behind. I insist that they spend at least one day a month going to museums or libraries, although people have funny ideas of what museums are about—I think they often start going too early and come out thinking that what is inside is dull, dead. I made a real drama of going as a student, and it was not until I left school that I went with no particular reason in mind and realized the beauty that was there. On the other hand, I try to get students to flip through magazines for things that might turn out to be useful—even if you find nothing in a magazine, you have not wasted any energy in looking and you fill the reservoir.

To work for an exhibition is incredibly exciting, and I love the emotional angle. It has something to do with the hope of seeing things that you have made in the setting you would like for them. All my pots are made for a fictitious room, which has in it only the thing I am making; it is a certain height and lit in a certain way. Galleries almost live up to the idea that in order to enable you to see anything the whole environment has to be grey, white, or whatever colour you decide, so that the only contrast is with the object you want to show. The disadvantage is that it all begins to seem a bit stagy. Because we live in such a cluttered world, or clutter it so badly ourselves, anything that is absolutely plain is suspect. If you painted everything grey, you would only have to explain it once, but the danger is that it would become overpowering, and everyone would get very intense about it.

I am never quite sure why people come to my exhibitions. They still expect to see bowls and domestic ware, though I have never made them much, certainly never shown them. The last exhibition was just as I wanted it, when it was all together. It was generally concerned with the way I thought about things. It was all to do with temples and sexual symbols, and it frightened the death out of most people. They did not talk about it,

Temples to Man, thrown and cut porcelain, celadon glazed, (front) pressed base.

mainly they just looked away. A common reaction was simply 'You cannot put feathers on pots', while it had seemed to me the obvious thing to do, put lots of very white feathers on a very small, shiny white pot.

I cannot control how people feel, I cannot even show them how I feel, because I am not sure. Which is why I make pots. I do it to try to explain to myself how I feel, or perhaps to get rid of it, rather than to communicate to people who may not understand in any case.

I know that many potters could make one of my pots, and I theirs—there are no secrets, pottery is not complicated—but to do so would not teach you

to look at things in a new way. What is difficult, and I would find impossible, is to make another potter's next pot. You cannot pick up on another kind of pottery, because it is rather like taking up somebody else's life. It is not that it would be imitation or anything, you are simply not able to do it. Sometimes you work on a parallel with someone else by chance, which is nice and rather crazy. Robin Welch once came to an exhibition of mine and said 'That's a shame, I was going to make some pots very like those.' We had made similar pots before, but when we talked about it, it turned out that our ways of making the same basic shape were very different.

If I had not made pottery, I should have been a sculptor, but I like the speed of ceramics. While I was making pots at Camberwell, there was a student from the sculpture department working outside with a kerbstone. I asked him if it was not supposed to be the hardest stone you could get. 'Yes' he said 'and I'm going to master it.' It was a lovely summer, and I could hear him out there every day for three months. At the end of that time he did not seem to have made much impression on the stone, and I asked him if it was not a bit of a waste of time. He said 'No, it's the rhythm I want to work in.' It took him about a year to finish one piece, and although I could see what he meant it would have driven me mad. I want to see it *now*. I do not think I am quick witted, but my ideas do change quite

Pots, thrown and cut in porcelain. Left: with pure silver, leather and wood.

drastically in a year. It depends on what I have seen and read. The more information you take in, the more your ideas are enlarged. Just as villains may turn out to be someone else's heroes, there is no wrong way of doing things, only the right way. When I make pots, I often dislike them, but a small part usually works. I make another version, retain the pot's good features and try to get rid of the bad, and I sometimes go on to make twenty, thirty, or even fifty pots. The ones that do not work tend to get destroyed. I find that they disappear—they always get broken somehow.

At one point, I tried to find out basically who I was when I first started working. All of my things are so diverse, there is no real connection between them, except me, and that's it—that's the connection. I arrive at situations and when I arrive I have almost finished. You can pick up with a pot, you can abuse it, and then you can throw it away, but you can always come back to it in a way which would be impossible with people. The trouble with the way I work is that I am never quite certain whether I have done what I wanted. I think I have, and perhaps six months later I decide that I was able to con myself because one element came out right. Again, I have selected what I wanted to see.

David Leach

David Leach joined his father's pottery at St Ives in 1930. After taking a technical course at North Staffordshire Technical College, he established the production of a range of stoneware at the Bernard Leach Pottery, where he stayed until the early 1950s. Since 1956, he has been running his own Lowerdown Pottery at Bovey Tracey, Devon, helped by his son Jeremy and several assistants. They produce sets of functional domestic ware, some with brushwork decoration. David Leach also produces his own individual pieces.

I was apprenticed not so much to my father as to the workshop, where I learned skills by working alongside people like Charlotte Epton, Muriel Bell and, later, Harry Davis, who was far more proficient as a thrower than I was. Even so, my father was always in the background, and we imbibed from him. After the war, I joined him for ten years of very productive partnership in which I acted as his assistant and interpreter. My father would sketch ideas for me to try out. Then, when we had agreed on the final design, I would show the samples to Bill Marshall, give him the specifications and watch over him for a while before he went on with the making. With a lot of standard shapes, though not all, my father would be the initiator and we would work them out together. In some ways, I may

Porcelain bowls, (left) 11 in. diameter and (above) 9 in. Brushed decoration and dots of red against blue washed ground; dolomite glaze.

have been more practical than he was, more aware of problems that might arise, because I had gone off to take a technical training.

In 1934, we had been asked by the Elmhirsts, who ran Dartington Hall, whether we could start a pottery department there. We were to make a range of domestic ware as well as individual pots, and I rather came to the conclusion that we had not enough experience between us to organize work on a larger scale than St Ives. Left at Dartington to think about it while my father went to Japan for fifteen months, I decided that it would be a good idea to go to Stoke-on-Trent to acquire more technical knowledge. Although industry was not the direction in which we wanted to work, I had a clear idea of what I wanted from the course. Knowing more about bodies, kilns, glazes, firing and that kind of thing, I felt I should be able to return to St Ives or to Dartington with new confidence. When I wrote to tell my father what I intended to do, he telegraphed back in a great hurry, misunderstanding the whole thing and believing that I had been seduced by industry. I think he felt that my ideas had not been sufficiently developed and that I was simply going up to Stoke to collect a lot of techniques that were not related to what we would be doing.

The concept of the pottery at Dartington had not been made entirely clear to us. I felt that the Elmhirsts and Bill Slater, the managing director, wanted my father there as a person of ideas and a figure, but we were uncertain whether the work itself was going to be done in a studio, a factory, or something in between. I saw it as an extension of St Ives, which would require technical abilities beyond those I had. Maybe, as an artist rather than a practical man, my father was less concerned. It would be natural for me to be anxious about certain aspects which would not bother him. However, I could not explain it all to him at that distance and, anyway, I went.

I returned in 1937 to carry on at St Ives. My father was away at Dartington by then, writing his *Potter's Book*, and I was free to run St Ives with all the new ideas I had developed at Stoke. It was then that I suggested that we should build up and train a skilled team of local workers, rather than depend on students passing through, to get the ware really established. I did not think of myself as a potential artist at all at that stage. I just thought I was a practical sort of bloke who was running a pottery and turning out a decent hand made ware. That's what I did and trained others to do.

Until 1937, all the people who were working in the pottery had been comers and goers, staying for a year, sometimes less. I maintained that to

Porcelain bowl, 10 in. diameter, with fluted decoration under pale Y'Ching type celadon glaze. Left: stoneware teapot, 1¾ pint capacity, off-white matt titanium glaze.

make a range of ware to a high standard we would have to depend on a skilled permanent staff. Through the headmaster of the local secondary school, I found boys who were willing to start a five or six year apprenticeship and that's when Bill Marshall started in 1938. This was really the beginning of what I call an organized and skilful production of standard ware.

With this permanent staff, the work went on smoothly. Students made their contribution, but we did not rely on them as we had before, whether they were there for six months or a year. The attitude was different. Local

boys of fifteen whose homes were within a quarter of a mile of the pottery could live economically and lacked the temptation to move away, whereas somebody coming down from the RCA would feel that he could survive a year in cheap digs in St Ives and go back to London when he had gained the workshop experience he wanted.

Stoke had given me an understanding of pottery materials that I had not had before. Of course, that was forty-odd years ago. We were pioneering in those days, I suppose, and we had nowhere to turn for relevant technical advice. There were only two or three other potters in the country doing our kind of work. There was little knowledge about pottery materials and how they might be expected to react under fire at different temperatures, or in different atmospheres.

At Stoke I learned pottery science and industrial technology in a form intended for industrial application and it was my business to translate this into our studio pottery terms. The information is now much more available from the art schools, so that few students wanting to become potters need to take the technical course I took. Nevertheless it helped me and I do not regret the time spent. Afterwards I entered into a very close relationship with my father for ten formative and stabilizing years, during which the pottery was also finding itself financially.

A great change took place over the war years. It had been very difficult for a studio potter to scratch a living before the war. In 1936, I remember, I took a couple of suitcases bulging with samples round Scotland, Wales and

all over the place in a battered two-seater Morris. I would be so pleased to have a five-pound order at the end of the day that I would telephone home. By the time the war ended, however, the big London stores were unable to obtain any of the industrial pottery with which they had been well stocked in prewar years; only white ware was available and it seemed very dull. A London buyer offered us at St Ives the chance of selling to her everything we made. That was a temptation to which we did not give way, as we were unwilling to be caught with only one outlet when industrial production revived, but it indicated the willingness of London stores to open their arms to the studio potters.

At the same time, there was a general movement towards creativity. The experience of war caused many people to take stock of their previous careers and accept the opportunity to make a new start. Some prisoners of war, for instance, who had developed artistic skills during captivity, settled down to an art school training after coming home. Development of the media and increased leisure combined with state-aided security and education to encourage an interest in the crafts.

Studio potters who were in production during the first two or three years after the war found a market through their introduction by the shops. If the public had seen and used studio ware, and could afford it, many of them

Porcelain bowl, 7 in. diameter, with engraved decoration under jade green celadon glaze. Porcelain box, 5 in. diameter with pink crackle, satin matt dolomite glaze.

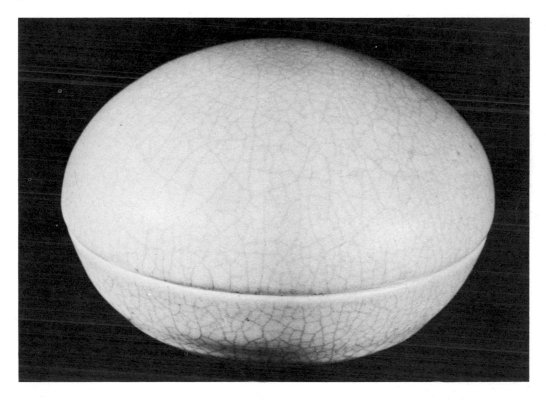

chose it and have not ceased to do so, despite the revival of industrial production in the late 1940s.

Although hand made functional work does command a higher price than that made industrially, if you are making something that will be subjected to everyday use there is a limit to what you can charge. When people are accustomed to paying £1.50 for a cup and saucer, they have to ask themselves whether they are prepared to pay more than £3 for one in my shop. I do not think you ask yourself the same question when you are choosing something that is not functional. Anything that may be considered an art object is out of the competitive field. The price is much more related to the maker's reputation. More and more potters now come into the sphere of fine art appreciation, selling their work in galleries. If they are doing fine work, I am all in favour of it, because there you can find a perfect combination of artistry and craftsmanship. I know there is an instinctive appreciation of a certain beauty—it is immediately apparent—but some of this work is very personal to the maker. It may have a stimulus, a provocation, but it does not often communicate with other people. In the confines of the functional field, the chances of communication are very much better, but people don't often want to be limited today.

On the other hand, few of us have the fertile imagination that can go on endlessly producing new ideas without any need for repetition. I have grown to accept that my kind of pottery must include repetitive work in which you arrive at a design, usually a functional shape, which you repeat in quantity, either yourself or with the assistance of colleagues, thus making your studio viable. You sell the work from your own showroom and to shops who resell it.

But if you stopped there, it would I think be death to one's creativity. I am not saying that the things made in this way are dead. Obviously once you have arrived at a design which satisfies you, then you go on making it. It is not that I and anyone who is working with me cease to be constantly critical. One can keep very alive in making things repetitively if one is really looking at them. Then it does not become mechanical—a possibility if you just concede to orders that people give you.

Every craftsman who is doing a good job can find a market; someone is going to come along with an order for a thousand. Is it my job as a hand craftsman to sit down and devote the time and energy to the thousand pots required? That would mean time and energy taken from a lot of other directions of creativity, and I don't think it is my job. Students in my workshop are doing this for me; goblets are being made to my design now, fifty of them, to meet such a need. A great deal of our making is of that kind although I am divesting myself of doing it personally, except in supervision. I think it is all right if it is providing someone with a training, but there is a limit—the difference between fifty mugs and a thousand. Fifty are done in a day, a thousand take much longer.

Stoneware vase, 9 in. high, thick oatmeal ash glaze over iron slip with iron spots.

DAVID LEACH

If you are going to accept an order for a thousand, why are you doing so? To make money. I contend that the craftsman has a greater responsibility to his creative context and potential. In my view, we must not fool ourselves that it is economically necessary to fill an order for a thousand. If I am a properly creative person, I retain a number of outlets for my energy and always leave the door open for fresh thinking—none of us makes enough opportunity for that. I know so many young people leaving art school and setting up workshops for the first time, economically fearful and dying for huge orders to cover their overheads, pay off their kilns. There is no harm in that if they know when to stop. One has to live economically, but once fairly confident of that, for goodness' sake keep your mentality alive by experimentation. I think you have to recognize such avenues of interest as glaze research or decorative effects without letting any single one seduce you into thinking it is all-important.

The fact that the craft is inexpensive in terms of materials and quick in terms of labour means that you can turn over ideas in your mind, translate them into clay and move on. Working with clay seems to appeal to the impulsive personalities; few potters want to labour painstakingly at the expense of spontaneity. They like to work with a material that responds quickly.

When I am working on something new and tentative, I sometimes help myself with a sketch. I do no drawing beforehand, but I have a blackboard and, when I reach a point where I am not clear about what the form should be, I might draw it in chalk before continuing at the wheel. The interaction between the blackboard and the wheel helps to project and clarify what is going on in my head.

If what you make is functional, your experiment might be the start of a new idea that will become repetitive. I can look down the range I have made here and pick out pots that began as one-offs. But, while you may consider a shape suitable for repetitive work because it is simple enough for someone else to make it from your prototype to the necessary standard for your catalogue range, it may not be the sort of thing that goes into an exhibition. The expectation of an exhibition is that the work is newer and more imaginative than that which constitutes your bread and butter, run of the mill.

This is something determined by the organizers of galleries and exhibitions, who sometimes go so far as to demand that the work shown will not have appeared elsewhere and, furthermore, will have been made within the last year. That sort of approach fails to recognize the difference between craftsman and artist. Many people deny a distinction, and I think they may be right in some ways, but most of us craftsmen who are living by our craft just do not live by making one-offs. We make a range of articles which we repeat, and I do not consider that an exhibition should be an occasion when a craftsman is shown in the wrong light as the maker of single works of art. There are many good craftsmen who are not creative artists, who

Fluted porcelain jar or tea caddy, 6½ in. high; jade green celadon glaze.

nevertheless make excellent livings through fine but undramatic work. That is craftsmanship.

Certainly, I find there is excitement in the way I work. I had an instance of it this morning: one of my porcelain eggs with a pink crackle in the glaze came out of the kiln with a blackish cloud over one side. This was not predetermined, it was given to me by the kiln. At first I reacted with a scowl, then a smile and, finally, approval. I know how the shadowed effect came about, but I should certainly be unable to arrange the areas where it occurred. This morning's example happened to be right. All along the line I do a lot of conscious experimentation, designing, mucking about with glazes, but at the same time the material and the firing conditions make suggestions to which I have to respond, possibly for future reference.

In Philip Trevelyan's film, Shoji Hamada has finished packing the kiln, all the pots are in, and he lights the fire. True to his Zen Buddhist background and observations, he has on the front of the kiln what amounts to an altar and sits for a moment in meditation. He is really saying, 'Look, I have done my bit and it is up to you, whoever you are.' It is an important feature of our kind of craft, which is not a science. There is another power at work and you have to submit to nature, you have to feel towards it. In an age of disbelief, Hamada represents an approach of humility.

My feeling for stoneware is heightened by just this element that is contributed by the flame. With earthenware, whatever you add in the way of decoration comes out starkly unchanged under the glaze, if it is fired in an electric kiln. Stoneware is transmuted by the heat; very often the thing that emerges is quite a lot removed from what you put down as decoration. This is the excitement of the high fire of stoneware, little seen at the lower temperature ranges.

I work from a knowledge of my materials and the limitations of my skills. To some extent, that confines my imagination, I admit. The idea is very important, and I think it should probably precede the detailed learning of technique. When I came back from Stoke I realized that I had attended a lot of lectures that had no bearing later. On the other hand, simply to learn a little technique, a little about the materials, and then go ahead is extremely amateurish. I feel it is important to achieve a balance between imagination, material and skill.

I am interested in the question of development, as opposed to big reactionary jump changes. I know I am a person who evolves very gradually. I cannot accept the casting off of tradition just to do one's own novel or original thing—that seems almost unintelligent. Although you must not be bound by tradition, you hurt yourself by failing to use what it can offer you.

It was not until 1953 that I began to realize that I had personally to develop as a potter. It would have been so easy, much easier, to break with my father if I had had strong convictions of my own that were at variance with his, but I liked his work. It was simply that I found my spirit inhibited by the domination of his. Janet must be the one person who has worked closely with him for a number of years without being visibly influenced. She is so strong in herself that she has maintained more independence than anyone else who has been as close to that dangerous fire, my father!

I think there is a danger with all the family following my father that we may not have done so for vocational reasons. My sons left school without academic qualifications and had an attractive craft on the doorstep. I have had to ask myself whether they each have the makings of a potter, or is it too easy for them? You can appreciate my father's contribution without making pottery in any way resembling his. He would be the last to approve of a pale imitation, wanting each of us to be ourselves. He often quotes a Chinese saying: 'He is a wise man who in his maturity makes full use of the gifts that he was born with.'

Stoneware dish, 16 in. diameter, matt, white dolomite glaze over tenmoku; wax resist.

Danka Napiorkowska & Roger Michell

Danka Napiorkowska and Roger Michell have a pottery in Malton, Yorkshire. Part of their time is taken up by organizing and designing for a slip casting unit which they started in November 1975 with several assistants. This is intended to give them the opportunity to make their own more elaborate thrown and turned pieces in underglaze painted earthenware.

Danka: We do not set out to make copies of eighteenth-century pottery, but we are particularly attracted to the qualities of that earthenware—the superb way it's made, its appearance, its feel, everything about it is so near perfection. Also, in a sense, it is very much more difficult to make than stoneware. You know that your work is going to be judged for its own qualities, and that you cannot rely on the kiln to transform an ash glaze. That's really terrific if it's your way of working, but we prefer to be more in control of our results.

Roger: We are sometimes asked if what we do is incomplete, because neither of us is alone responsible for the whole pot. In the eighteenth century, making and decorating were thought of entirely separately, and it does not seem in the least incongruous that one of us should be dealing with one particular aspect of the pot, especially as the discipline of decoration seems entirely different from that of actually making the pot.

Pieces from Walking day service and Long John Silver teaset.

Danka: It is not necessarily that Roger does not think about decoration, or that I do not consider the making of shapes.

Roger: When I make a pot, I regard the decoration as a finishing touch, while Danka's attitude is quite different—she sees it as a blank surface on which to begin painting. When my enthusiasm is waning, Danka's is just starting. The combination usually works well.

The industrial revolution affected pottery in the mid eighteenth century, but was industrial only in the sense that people worked in factories set up in such pottery centres as Liverpool, Staffordshire, West Yorkshire and Bristol, normally established centres of delft manufacture since the seventeenth century. As the ware was made by resident and journeyman potters, it is possible to find Lambeth and Liverpool delft that has clearly been painted by the same hand. The activity inside these newly established factories depended entirely on hand craft, since it was not until the 1820s that jigger and jolley machinery and slip moulding became a common method of manufacture. The craft skills developed over this period were among the most sophisticated technically and best applied aesthetically in the history of pottery and porcelain. So that those we look back at for standard—Astbury, Whieldon, Wedgwood—were engaged exclusively in a hand process.

Although it was a vicious capitalist age, the result was constructive: what was made, especially in the period of neoclassical design, was very much geared to what the market wanted. Creamware was intended as utilitarian

DANKA NAPIORKOWSKA & ROGER MICHELL

Tableware, thrown and turned, with press-moulded turtles; hand painted under lead glaze.

crockery, but the whole point was that it was the first product that was going to the middle classes. In a sense, the creamware encouraged a lifestyle, as well as responding to the requirements of a particular class. Until that time, there had been fairly primitive pottery, or imported blue and white ware which was wildly expensive.

In America, anyway, porcelain and 'china' are still very important, while pottery is not. It seemed a terrific achievement to get our earthenware into the Cartier ceramics department.

Danka: The distinction very definitely exists. I am designing some patterns at the moment for tableware that will be sold in America, fairly cheaply and in large numbers, but they would not dream of producing them on earthenware—it has to be bone china. It makes a change for me, and bone china is really very good to drink out of.

As it applies to me, earthenware demands certain qualities in decoration, because my designs for bone china will all be done in another factory once my drawing has been to the printer—that is all I do, whereas the approach with earthenware is much more direct—I actually paint every single pot.

When we go on to do our own porcelain later this year, I want to use etching as a decorative technique, to print on paper from an etched copper plate and transfer the design to the pot, really approaching it from a print-making point of view. When we start making porcelain, all my pieces will probably be flat, not curved, and I cannot tell yet whether the work that we do together will have etched or hand painted decoration—it may turn out to be a combination of both. The sort of etching that I do, or have done in the past, has a similarity in feeling to the pottery in that it tends to be finely drawn and rather precise.

Roger: You could transfer print earthenware as easily as porcelain, but I think the strength and delicacy of porcelain should be brought into the design. Hopefully, the porcelain will be fairly detailed and still highly decorated. It has such a beautiful glaze quality that you could draw on it in enamel with a pen, doing delicate drawings and washes of enamel. While enamel can appear a bit shiny and gross on earthenware, its effect on porcelain is much more subdued because it inherits the qualities of the glaze underneath. The depth of an earthenware glaze turns to your advantage in other techniques—with lustre, for example, you almost become aware of shadows between the lustre and the body.

The work that we do together is not normally planned as a whole. I have made a few pots using Danka's shapes, like the walking teaset, but shapes are, in general, disciplined by how you can do it. Earthenware is not a good throwing body—you cannot get a tremendous amount of shape. It is no coincidence that eighteenth century shapes are as they are. With a body of the kind that they would be likely to use at that time you tend to throw a cylinder and make your shape near to that, because the body is not inherently strong enough to move far from it. Earthenware jugs normally have a wide base and a rim of the same width, while the middle leaves the cylinder shape only very slightly. Even the coffee pots, apparently very fluid, derive much of their shape from the foot, which is turned, while the curve of the sides departs only slightly from the straight line. In many ways, the discipline actually contributes to the elegance.

Many of our shapes are determined by the capabilities of the clay. The bottom half of a globular teapot is mainly turned, and the top is an even dome, which has its own inherent structure and holds together very well.

Cheese dish and coffee pot. Hand painted in blue and brown and (right) silver lustre.

Tea set, thrown and turned with press-moulded birds.

The camel teapot is thrown in two pieces, base and cylinder, and joined together.

Danka: With our more complicated shapes, details such as the fish are modelled, and Roger then makes a fairly simple mould in which the clay is pressed. That is how the feet were first made. You can work very quickly by combining thrown and moulded pieces. It is a good, direct method and forms the basis of all our hand made work.

Roger: I love throwing, but by itself it is fairly limited, and the way in which we combine it with press moulding seems to work very well. Hand building as a technique would not suit earthenware, which is difficult to stick together at the best of times—the edges tend to dry apart, and pieces crack.

Danka: Underglaze colours have their limitations, too—the palette is restricted, and a lot of the colours that you buy on the market share the chemical formulae of the original pigments, but lack life in comparison. You have to grind them and add extra ingredients, but some remain unpleasant to use. I have probably bought every single underglaze colour on the market, and I use the ones that I like most and that I find work best. There are always some combinations that work incredibly well—certain

DANKA NAPIORKOWSKA & ROGER MICHELL

browns, greens and blues are always marvellous together and are, in fact, quite eighteenth-century in feeling. The good thing about underglaze painting is that it is much more a part of the pot than enamel, which can appear an afterthought as it lies on the surface. I often lay colours on top of each other, and that is difficult with hand-painted enamel. I also find underglaze easier to use, but that may be because I am used to it and have worked out a very quick technique. I work out roughly what I am going to do, perhaps drawing the shape of a curve, but that is all, the rest is freehand. You can more or less predict how the finished work will look, although the colours change in the firing. The challenge lies in the need to be very precise; if you make a mistake you cannot erase it—your only hope is to cover it up, but that is not always possible.

Roger: We like to feel that most of our work is intended for a particular sort of use, like the walking teaset for breakfast, the duck and the elephant pots

Captain Munro and Tippoo's Tiger sauce-boat, slip cast and hand painted under glaze.

for drinking gin out of, and the dinner-for-two casseroles as a token of affection.

Danka: A lot of those were sold as wedding presents—a very obvious sort of use.

Roger: The pots are useful, but useless, too—although they all work, one doubts that some of the more elaborate will ever be used. There is no concept of making an object whose function is critical to it. We have in mind an additional purpose of amusing or pleasing somebody. That seems to me the reason why people started embellishing what they made. The idea that design must be limited to the requirements of function seems spurious when you can increase the enjoyment to be got out of using your work by turning it into a fat man—I think it more than justifies making a teapot in that shape. In the tradition of eighteenth-century Chelsea soup tureens made in the form of cabbages, there was no problem about aesthetics—you made them in order to please and amuse somebody else, which adds an extra dimension to a functional object. A teapot is a fairly incidental part of one's life and can be treated with flippancy.

It seems to me that to make design a moral and social question is to misread the whole situation—people really use design as an accessory to their lives. There is a danger that you might try to give a material, a medium, and an object like a teapot something that they ought not to have, and turn pottery into a symbol of right mindedness. There comes a point when people limit their field so tightly that they feel it wrong to put on decoration, or add to the shape. Ultimately, there are so many rules that development is not possible.

What we are doing started partly as a reaction. It also strikes me as a shame that some of the industrial producers have climbed on the back of the studio pottery movement. The effect has been to devalue studio work by mimicking its vocabulary.

Danka: On the other hand, Stoke-on-Trent is much maligned, especially in art schools. Having taught in a couple of colleges, I am amazed that, apart from one brief trip in three years to look at a few factories, students have little or no contact with industry at all. There is so much you can learn, and so much help available there. Fortunately the situation is beginning to change, though slowly. Perhaps the trouble is that whereas industry, when it was established, was controlled by designers, and the innovators were the people who succeeded, things have changed so that the salesmen are the designers.

Roger: Our objective in starting our own casting unit was to leave us the time and freedom to make our own work. We only make about two hundred slip-cast pieces a week, probably no more than twenty of any one design.

Danka: We aim to keep to this volume, making more complicated and exciting shapes. The point is that we do not want to turn out work indiscriminately—I do not know of any other pottery of our size making comparable slip-cast ware.

DANKA NAPIORKOWSKA & ROGER MICHELL

Cow in the Bath butter dish, slip cast earthenware, hand painted under glaze.

Roger: The success of the walking teasets almost became a problem; the demand was enormous almost at once, and we enjoyed ourselves for a year, but we were making five or six sets a week, squeezing other work around it. For that reason we sold the design to Carltonware on a royalty basis. In fact, we are still making pieces in the casting unit, but we have not done any by hand for nine months or so.

We decided not to take any further part in the industrial production of the teaset, although the design has been changed in subtle ways, and we feel the finish to be a bit gross. To remain responsible for the quality would have complicated our lives too badly.

Danka: We have been very lucky in the ease with which that teaset transferred from throwing and turning to slip casting. The techniques are very different. We also realized, when we first started slip casting last November, that we could not adapt any of our existing designs but the duck and the elephant teapots from making by hand.

Little Willie teapot, homage to Donald McGill, slip cast and hand painted.

Roger: The designs for our casting unit are very definitely made with the method in mind, but I am surprised at how little the technique limits what is produced. It is quite sophisticated enough to provide a high degree of freedom—what you cannot actually mould in one piece, you can cut up into its component parts, moulding them separately—marvellous for elaborately modelled pieces like Captain Munro, Little Willie, or the cow. There seems to be more point in slip casting them than a circular teapot, say, which you could throw and turn just as quickly. The unit was, after all intended to take the pressure off the hand making—by the time you have thrown your first dozen pots to pay for your studio, the next dozen so that you can eat, you have little time left for new work, or something experimental. As soon as we decided to start slip casting, people kept asking if we were going to make certain pieces more cheaply. That was not the point at all; we did not intend to use one technique in attempting to reproduce another.

Bryan Newman

Bryan Newman works with his wife Julia and usually one assistant at their pottery in Langport, Somerset. He produces a consistent range of domestic stoneware as well as slab-built pieces of ceramic sculpture which are often based on architectural forms.

I went to art school all set to be a painter. At the end of a general course in art which took about two years, I was going to be a sculptor. Right at the eleventh hour, I changed my mind again and decided on ceramics. I think I was attracted by the breadth of the subject, for not only did it concern pots and utilitarian items, it could also be sculpture, or just like painting in the case of tile panels and mosaics. I felt I could have all these means of expression simply by being a potter. At that stage, I had not considered whether I would be able to earn my bread at it; I was doing it for its own sake and for the personal satisfaction I could get out of it, and only much later did I realize that a living could actually be made. Pottery is one of the better activities in that respect. If you are a painter, you are either very successful or you fall flat on your face.

After a year spent with the Forestry Commission as an alternative to army service, I went back to London and worked in Richmond Park for a year so that I could teach one day a week at Camberwell. Later I became a technical assistant there, too, and it was arranged that I could spend half the time on my own work, I had started making sculptural pieces by that time, about seven years after I had actually started potting. A whole new generation had started there and I had been pushed aside, in a sense, because as a student I had been the golden boy. So I was searching for something that would put me back on the map.

One Saturday afternoon, I was very dissatisfied with a bottle I was making. I cut it up, and when I put it back together again it turned into a cactus. Making two or three more, I realized that a new field had opened up, and people began to take notice of me again. As I wanted to exhibit somewhere, Lucie Rie, who had arrived at Camberwell while I was away, suggested that I contact Henry Rothschild at Primavera. He bought seven pieces off me and rang about two months later to offer me an exhibition with Ian Auld, another hand builder. I took six months or so to prepare about fifty sculptural pieces for that exhibition, and I must have made about £300. That, plus my savings, gave me enough to start up my first studio with three other potters in London in 1959.

Most of the time I enjoyed teaching, but I found that it took a lot out of me—it's giving all the time. It was only at Harrow that I felt my batteries were being charged rather than flattened. In all, I had been teaching for about fifteen years by the time I gave it up. I think most art schools are places where people go to make up their minds what they want to be. They have a vague idea, as I had, 'I'm going to be a painter' or something, but do not really know what being a painter involves. This is awfully painful for the teacher—he is responsible for both the very enthusiastic and the very bored who are using the two years to delay making up their minds. Then there are the in-betweens, who really can be helped. Those who are no good you can't do anything with, and the very good ones grasp it all through looking. At Harrow, where the students were all going to work as potters, most were dedicated and, in that case, the better the students, the more you could give them.

I have learned a lot from many other potters. Yes, I am always pinching ideas, but I feel that I've got more from architects. I often seem to go back to architecture, or engineering in the case of the bridges, say. I think the variety of my pots makes me the Berlioz of the ceramics movement. I have a finger in every pie that I can put it in. I like exploring new ideas or thoughts I have not had for some time. I find the banal, the insignificant, the ordinary just as fascinating in a way as the brilliant and the remarkable.

Pottery does enable you to make sculpture on a domestic scale. I like that side of it. I think that is why I manage to sell sculptural pieces, people can

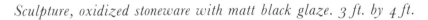

Sculpture, oxidized stoneware with matt black glaze. 3 ft. by 4 ft.

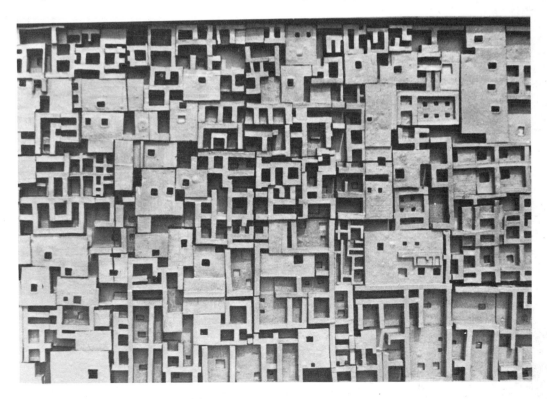

BRYAN NEWMAN

actually fit them into their homes. At one time, I almost went on to architectural ceramics. I did a doorstep for a Cork Street art gallery in London, a plaque for a private customer, and two pieces about eight feet by four for the Stork hotel in Liverpool. It was getting bigger and bigger, approaching the size I was starting to delight in. I should love to do something really enormous—the thing I feel missing from my life is a tile panel a hundred feet high, or some giant piece of sculpture.

For an exhibition, I like to produce, say, twelve pieces rather than work hard for six months on one show. I've been in a lot of group exhibitions, which I like very much. In one of them, wanting my contribution to have a feeling of totality, I did only teapots. I started off with common table teapots and they gradually became more and more like tea engines. They would make tea, but they were definitely mechanical. All along the line you could see steps from utilitarian to non-functional. In the end, the teapot part diminished and the sculptural element took over; the last was an enormously elaborate handle with the body of the teapot completely atrophied—by that time it was pure sculpture. Seeing it isolated, no one would ever realize that it arose from the idea of a teapot. Later, I also made squashed teapots, giant teapots, and an Islamic teapot that looks like a minaret. The variations illustrate an idea I find appealing, that words have no boundaries. Even the simplest words merge into one another.

I have made a lot of ceramic boats that came from sailing, really, but also from the stickleback. First of all, I am fond of sticklebacks, and I could

Edwardian high-rise, slab built and carved in reduced stoneware. Teapots, dipped in glaze and coloured slip.

not conceive of a way to turn the shape into clay. In the end, I decided that my favourite characteristic was the way in which the tail dwindles almost to nothing and suddenly flares into a little fan shape. What I did was chop the head off altogether. I slab built it so that it came out square, though I kept the feature that I really thought was marvellous. But it looked like a tree, and that started trees going. Then I saw that if I cut the top off the tree, I turned it into a bush with no pedestal of trunk below it. The bush then elongated itself into a poplar, and at that point I took the whole of the technique I had developed through my slab building and cutting clay to a sharp edge, and made a boat out of it. Again, I had tried to make boats a long time before, without having evolved the right way to do it. Now, how-ever, I had the technique. I cut the clay leather hard—it is a matter of getting it in just the right state if you want very thin feathery edges. The tool to use is a paint scraper, not a knife. The blade is so wide that you have full control when cutting through the clay with the sharpened sides.

I made boats for about three years before I saw that by turning them up-side down I could make bridges. That delighted me. Then the bridges grew more arched and turned into doorways. The chess sets that I made

Arks, slab built and carved in reduced stoneware.

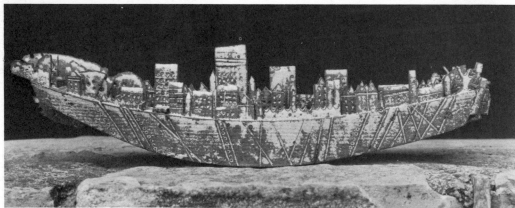

Trees (left) thrown, one with glazed base, and (right) slab built and carved in reduced stoneware.

were offshoots of the boats' superstructures. They turned into tombstones or people—peopled landscapes at one point. They became very crowded. Things had started off very simple and became increasingly complex, until I had to give them up because they were so elaborate.

The same technique that came out of the stickleback-trees went into the landscapes that turned into towns. I did slices of land at one time and then went on to population. Villages grew into small towns and then to big industrial cities; often, the nucleus of church and village green remained, surrounded by Victorian flats, then boxes—council flats and high rise offices—with factories and estates. Communications went on by road, rail, canals and sea.

When I got to the stage in my slabwork at which everything was very tight and ornate, I went on to big, simple, undulating slabs. You bend them quickly and let them set. Then you put three or four together. The technique is rather hit and miss, but those that combine well give me something.

Maybe, in the first year, I would have carried out a commission I did not like, because I am a survivor. It is important to be able to live. What is fortunate about pottery is that anyone who can exist through the first years of struggle can then choose more and more what he wants to do because there is so much work. The problem is not selling pottery but actually making it.

BRYAN NEWMAN

I sell a quarter of my work to individuals and the rest to shops. Most shops come on a cash and carry basis. They choose the pots they want, we pack them, they pay me, and that's the end of it. I think the whole of my life is devoted to making things simple. You can cram more in if everything works simply and efficiently. I enjoy running a business. I even like doing the paperwork and balancing the books.

I use a fairly stable clay which has stayed much the same for a number of years, because a change in the clay often has ramifications all along the line. We do keep bringing glazes in and phasing others out. I think I now have a range from very shiny to very dry for use on reduced stoneware fired at 1300°C. They are begged, borrowed, stolen, developed, modified. I now have a recipe book, which I reviewed for 'Craftwork'. It even has a colour chart. From the glazes I have tried so far, it looks as if I am going to get quite a few new ones from it. Some potters are secretive about their glazes, although I think on the whole potters are very open about everything. I suppose some of them feel that if you have struggled hard and taken a long time to achieve a certain effect, for some student to come along and get it just for the asking is a bit unfair.

I work with Julia, but she normally makes her pots and I make mine. Sometimes we decorate each other's work, and we occasionally fool people by using one another's shapes. Then there is a guy working for us. We tend to have assistants for half a year. That is part of the search for variety. We like working by ourselves, but we also like working with other people. We go out to the workshop around nine o'clock and usually stop between five and

Undulating slab forms in reduced stoneware.

six That seems to happen day after day. You find a rhythm and stick to it. I like working about seven hours and I do it fairly intensely. Except when I start arguing. I think I hire my assistants for their ability to argue.

I like assistants either to know a lot about pottery, so that I can simply set them to work on their own, or to know nothing at all, when they can learn a lot from doing all the very basic jobs. Between those alternatives, they want to learn to throw, and you tend to be giving them more in the way of teaching than you are getting out of them.

The very sad thing is that so many people are after jobs in pottery. I would say I had written to about forty people this year to say 'Sorry, no work'. I am sure I am not alone in that. Talk to any potter—they are continually turning people away. I think they want to work for us with a

Casserole, thrown in stoneware, iron glaze down to shoulder, dry surface below.

BRYAN NEWMAN

view to setting up on their own eventually. A lot come from colleges, but quite a few have been working at some other jobs for four or five years. They decide to give up what they call the rat race and make a fresh start in pottery. I had one guy who first started as a police cadet and worked in a bank for a couple of years until that began to get at him then, while recovering from a nervous breakdown, did pottery as occupational therapy.

The quality of work somehow depends on when you see it and how you feel at the time. I think you can be for things in the morning and against them in the afternoon. And they can mean something one day and be totally meaningless the next. I throw away very few unsuccessful pots. In a way, I think your bad pots subsidize the good. I like people to realize what they're getting, though, and if I am selling something as a second, I insist that it's known to be substandard and the customer can see what is wrong with it. It still has a certain value—it may be quite a nice pot with a split in it, or a little bit of bloating. I am not fanatical in that way, and my table ware is done in the same spirit as the sculpture, really.

Industrial pottery is as much for show as studio ceramics. It fits into a different sense of values, but I think they are just as aesthetic in a way. I

Townscape, slab built and carved in reduced stoneware.

Tea engine, thrown and hand built in stoneware.

don't think all manufacturers say to themselves, 'I'm going to make a bomb of money out of this and I don't care what it looks like.' However, if you really analyse a lot of industrial pottery, it doesn't all work as beautifully as one might hope. I do like functional ware to function, though if a teapot is particularly endearing, I am sometimes willing to forgive it a dribble because of the pleasure it gives. At one time, when I was a student, industrial pottery was anathema to me. I hated it and could not see how anyone might think it had feeling. Now I delight in it.

I am not a rustic potter. At ceramic symposiums, people start talking about the iniquities of industry. They have all come by train or car, most of them watch television or go to the cinema. Except for the pottery, their lives depend in some way on industry. Yet, for some reason they make it the fall guy, the baddy. Maybe we deserve the fey reputation as a group, because we do rail against modern civilization, while at the same time living in it. It would be very difficult to keep out of it.

Craftsmanship passing from generation to generation and a feeling for the integrity of the peasant are part of what is, I think, basically an intellectual movement. You do not take up pottery because your father has

Bridge, horizon and strip development, slab built and carved. Right: minarets, hand built with thrown details.

done it. One is a potter today like one is a painter or a sculptor, and the thing that distinguishes potters' work from that of say an architect or a film director is that they do it on their own. I come from a family of shopkeepers really and I have a little business, so I suppose in that way I am carrying on the family tradition.

Siddig A. El'Nigoumi

Siddig A. El' Nigoumi, working in the African tradition, coils earthenware pots which he finishes with burnishing and engraved decoration. His other work consists mainly of press-moulded dishes, some in stoneware with slip trailing and some using his burnished earthenware technique. He works and teaches at Farnham Art School.

When I was a child, we used to spend our school holidays in a small village by the White Nile about three hundred miles from Khartoum. Every summer (the rainy season) we used to play by a pond just outside the village, making toys, animals and so on out of clay. I was mad about steam trains. I used to love the way you could see the whole train from the last carriage as it rounded a bend. I particularly remember making an engine and carriages from the dry roots of papyrus. I gave them clay wheels on wooden axles and, of course, when I pulled my train along the rails I had made, also in clay, it fell off as it came to a curve. Playing by the pond for many years, I grew to love clay and the feel of it.

One of our other activities was to search for storage jars that had been buried in shifting sand. As long as there had been a village in the district, it was the custom to store dry rations and water in jars half buried in the ground. The wood and straw houses only last for three to five years before they are rebuilt some distance away, so that we had no way of telling where pots might have been left. As children we used to dig for them and break them open in the vain hope of finding treasure. Now that I am a potter, I regret not having carefully preserved the pots because they were covered with beautiful, simple decoration. Later, when I visited the village, I collected pottery fragments. Perhaps they were the very ones we left in the sand more than thirty years ago.

My next encounter with clay was at teachers' training college in Dilling, West Sudan, where I was a student. They happened to have pottery equipment and our art teacher showed us how to use the wheel, although being a painter he did not know very much about throwing. We found it quite impressive, but did not get to use it much because we had other things to do. At that time, I was very keen on sculpture. I used to carve soft wood that I brought in from the forest nearby.

The area is mountainous and the people are poor. All sorts of crafts go on, from beadwork, basket making and pottery to the construction of enormous

Left: YEAP POH CHAP. Porcelain bottle, after Chinese style, with yellow crackle glaze, decorated with impressed seal.

H

SIDDIG A. EL'NIGOUMI

carriers for the harvest out of wood plastered with cow dung, about half an inch thick and light enough to be carried on the head. Village women coil rather sandy clay to make round-bottomed storage pots, and water jars with very simple decoration, that they sell in the market place. There was nothing of that in my home town, Khartoum, except perhaps for the ivory and ebony carvings which are made for the tourists, some crudely made water jars (zeers) and coffee pots, and other small town crafts.

The students used to go out of Dilling together on treks, visiting places of interest in different parts of the country. We all collected material for a team project on which we had to write a report. As we had no means of printing, we had to select the student with the best calligraphy to write it out in Arabic. This task had fallen to me several times over the two years and when the college was invited to send someone to work on children's

Elephant box, hand built and modelled in grogged stoneware with incised decoration. Candle holder, about 20 in. high, modelled in stoneware. Coiled pot in burnished red earthenware, incised pattern. Press-moulded dish, Message, trailed slip.

Press-moulded stoneware dish, Dsougi, with trailed slip decoration.

magazines in the Publications Bureau in Khartoum I was offered the place. I was trained to carry on from the calligrapher there in the early 1950s. I did some illustration and I enjoyed calligraphy. Meanwhile, I found that I was interested in art, and was released in 1952 to go to the art school on condition that I should either teach or return to the Publications Bureau at the end of the course. We continued to go on treks, but this time the reports were printed with wood engravings and linocuts. After finishing the three-year course, I was nominated to stay on as a pottery student teacher.

Two years later I came to the Central School of Arts & Crafts, where I soon started to take pottery seriously, with sculpture as my second subject. Now some of my work is related to sculpture, though it is in clay. I feel I can trust the material and it trusts me—I gained confidence in clay so early in my life that I think it has become a part of me. When you are doing sculpture in clay, you are adding, rather than chipping away as you do with stone or wood. I like the sense of growth.

When I went back to teach at the art school in Sudan, I was worried at the prospect of teaching the stylistic points that I had learned in England. I started by looking at what the students had been doing in the way of shapes and saw a single idea, the traditional water pot, sometimes with a foot, though that had not been needed in the past because the pot would rest in a depression in the sand. I took my classes to the Ethnographical Museum in Khartoum, telling them to forget what the objects were and to concentrate on the shape, whether it was a wooden article, a pot, a basket or a spear. Every student had a sketchbook and we started working from there, analysing all the shapes. I had been afraid that the experiment might not work, but the result was exciting, not only to me but the students too, as they found many forms that adapted well to pottery. From then on, whenever they got stuck, the students went back to the museum to look for new ideas. No matter how creative you are, you come to a halt and have to find something fresh and inspiring.

As time went by, I was grateful for the technique I had learned in England. I appreciated the discipline of throwing teapots and casseroles as the Central School then required us to do. The feeling at that time, the late 1950s and early 1960s, was towards industrial design and I found myself experimenting with European methods of casting to produce a coffee pot in a traditional Sudanese form. On the other hand, there was a lot I had to unlearn because it did not suit Sudan at all.

I realized that I needed to look for inspiration locally and I was interested in adapting other kinds of art to pottery: painting, calligraphy and the incising of texture or pattern, as well as carving and relief building. At

Earthenware coffee pot, slip cast, inspired by (left) traditional Sudanese form.

SIDDIG A. EL'NIGOUMI

the Central School, I moulded a flattish dish with the idea that this would provide a good surface on which to practise my other ways of expressing myself. One of the methods of decoration that I used was a European technique; although scratched decoration is traditionally African, to fill the scratches with iron oxide or to trail slip are not. It suited me to employ these techniques, but using my own style as an artist potter.

Burnishing is something that occurred to me in England. I started it about five or six years ago, inspired by a traditional Sudanese coffee pot. It is essential both to have the right kind of clay and to start smoothing at the right moment, just when it is leather hard, or the water continues to evaporate from the clay, killing the burnish. On the other hand, the clay must not be dried too fast; it must dry naturally, far away from any source of heat. In making my biscuit-fired animal lanterns, I throw the component pieces individually before joining them together and then burnish the surface with spoons of various sizes. All the clay particles are pushed together with the bowl of a spoon to give a smooth effect. If burnishing is to be embellished by scratched decoration, the clay has to be left to dry completely before scratching, otherwise you fail to achieve a clear colour contrast. I am also experimenting with a burnished surface, biscuit fired to 800 C, over which I burn newspapers in order to give it a range of colours from light browns, dark browns to black.

The decoration I use has something to do with homesickness. I have been in England for eight years and I think I was most homesick during the first

Dish, Karima, scratched decoration. Lantern, thrown and hand built.

five. There are still moments when I am walking down the street by myself and my thoughts are far away from Farnham. The whole Nubian area of Sudan, which is now flooded by the Nile above the Aswan Dam, was so rich in decoration. The women, children and old men who remained when the men left to find work had little land to cultivate and occupied themselves by decorating their mud houses with local materials, such as ball clays and colouring oxides, which they obtained from the hills near the villages. Other vegetable colours were bought from the village shop. Originally the homes were decorated only for celebrations, but gradually the craft developed until the houses were completely decorated inside and out. There was no fear of its destruction by the weather, as rainfall in the area is almost nil. The excellent photographs taken by Marian Wenzel for her book *House Decoration in Nubia* (Duckworth, 1972) were collected as the last of the inhabitants were being evacuated to settlements inside the Sudan and Egypt, and show only a fraction of what was there, but they did refresh my memory of what I had seen. I felt it was the least I could do to record some impressions of this decoration in my own work. The houses were made of green bricks plastered with sand, and I am working in clay, which seems the natural alternative.

Mary Rogers

Mary Rogers has a studio at her home in Loughborough and concentrates on the exploration of natural forms. She makes individual pieces finely hand-built in pinched porcelain which is sometimes coloured with precisely applied specks of pigment.

As soon as I started to work with clay I knew that it was the material I'd been looking for. I concentrated on building by hand, and from the beginning pottery has been, for me, a form of imaginative expression rather than a desire to make vessels. Building things slowly and quietly by hand is a way of exploring the natural world in clay for which I do not think the wheel would be as sensitive. Quick methods of making do not really interest me anyway—it is in the slow building and refining and decorating of a form that I find the enjoyment. The rhythm of making pieces in the hands tends naturally towards a bowl, a hollow, a cave—the walls enclose space and so are containers. A hollow shape is rich in symbolism and association; it is a basic natural form.

Since childhood I have kept natural history collections, and my work has been based on natural forms from the first piece I made. At that time, in 1960, people who saw the work thought it an eccentric approach, and I used to have to explain and defend it in the talks which I gave to colleges, evening groups and schools. The difficulty was in accepting that by a pot you might mean something without any necessary claim to function. This seems strange now that a free approach is almost the rule rather than the exception.

I feel that my initial training and some years' work as a calligrapher have been invaluable in my work as a potter. One is involved in assessing correct curves, balance and spacing, and the outward turn of a good serif is very like the curve of a rim. In fact, part of the pleasure to be had from a well formed and decorated pot is very like that from a well formed letter and well spaced word.

My ceramics were first exhibited in 1961 in Nottingham, when my work was selected for the Midland Group of Artists, and all my small output went there for four or five years. I didn't actually show in London until 1965, and I am pleased that I waited, because as soon as more people saw my work I had many requests for pieces, which I would not have been able to supply had my children been as young as they were when I had the first

Pinched and hand built porcelain: Leaf form (1975) and Spreading Peacock (1974) dotted with coloured oxides; Peeling Birch (1975)

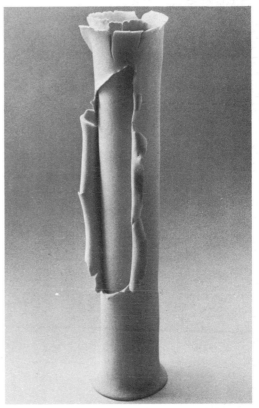

MARY ROGERS

White Wave (1975) pinched and hand built in white porcelain.

exhibition. The time which I have been able to devote to potting has increased as they have grown up.

The forms of my early coiled stoneware pieces were chunky and resembled carved stones. They reflected my interest in the shapes of rocks and boulders, and the patterns of fossils and erosion found in them. Then, partly as a reaction, and also as a challenge, I wanted to make more delicate work. I was teaching ceramics at a College of Education at the time and when drawing bark patterns with the students and discussing how these might be translated into clay I realised that one really needed a translucent material for the delicate curling shapes. Curling, crumpled, flowing forms were beginning to excite me visually very much. I had a marrow-end that had dried into a marvellously crunched shape, and the complex irregularity of the folds was fascinating after the more regular structure of the fossils and rocks which had absorbed me up till then. At the same time, my husband was writing a book on sculpture, and we had become very interested in the shapes of drapery. I felt that I needed to be able to use clay in a way which had these fluid qualities, and the convoluted folds in many of my pieces were made for these reasons. There were other reasons of course. Hopefully, a piece will evoke many different things with similar qualities, hint at many different sources, make visual metaphors, not merely reproduce one thing; otherwise it does not stir the imagination.

I started to make porcelain in order to get this delicacy and movement, and once you have made porcelain, it is so lovely when it does work that you fall in love with its qualities. Stoneware comes out of the kiln pretty well as you intended, without warping or slumping or any of the things that can happen to porcelain during the firing. Porcelain has something of a life of its own, and presents more of a challenge. It has such a lovely purity, and of course the translucency. It made it possible for me to capture the qualities of many of the things which I had been collecting for years, such as shells and dried pods, and seaweeds and feathers—delicate things which the light passes through, where space is defined by layers of fine material superimposed. So I started to design with light and shadow in mind.

All of my porcelain is pinched, which is one of the oldest ways of making pots, probably the earliest, because it is so instinctive. Anyone with a piece of clay will probably start pinching it without thinking. There is something exciting about working in the simplest, earliest techniques. You start with a lump of clay and press your thumb into the middle, pinching round and round gently. It is amazing how fine the clay can become, pinched until there is almost nothing between your finger and thumb. The direct handling of the clay, coaxing it to do what I want, not imposing myself too much,

Convoluted Bowl (1975), pinched in white porcelain.

but working gently with it, is very important to me. You have to work with relaxed concentration, receptive to the forms which the clay is happy to take. Fine porcelain dries out quickly in the warmth of your hands, and I often hold it in my hands, particularly with a difficult shape, until it is stiff enough to maintain its form without support. As you pinch more finely, unless you ease in the excess whilst working, you obviously get more clay widening out like a fan, and it is with this that I make the folds of the 'convoluted bowls'. I rest the bigger pieces in a cradle of foam rubber, inside any basin which is larger than the piece itself, and shore them up with more pieces of foam rubber. As the pots dry I pull out the pieces of foam from the convolutions. I enjoy working out the answer to technical and creative problems. It sometimes takes a long time to find the solution, and then, when you have done so, it seems so obvious that you can't imagine why you did not think of it before.

I work mostly in my lap, but I use a turntable to turn the pot round for a comprehensive view; I have a mirror in the studio for this reason. It is part of the old lettering training—when working on lettering I used to hold it up

to a mirror so that I could see the faults more objectively, without reading the shapes as a word. The mirror now comes in useful in the pottery when the pot is to be placed on a footring. I make this by rolling out a piece of clay, trimming it into a strip and joining the ends together; I balance the pot on the ring in front of the mirror, so that I can assess it from more than one viewpoint at once. This is necessary because a pot which is hand-built is always slightly asymmetrical—that can be part of its charm and individuality—so that the best place for the foot is not necessarily in the centre; it has to be discovered by moving the pot around until the perfect point of balance is found. When this is determined, I mark the position of the ring on the base of the pot and join it on with slurry.

When the pots are absolutely dry, I scrape them with a razor blade or a steel kidney to refine the form, and at the same time remove the finger marks, which I feel break up the surface by catching the light in an unintended way. Also, I like a form to look as though it has grown from within,

Spiralling Bowl, painted with coloured oxides, and (opposite) Opening Flower (1975).

and dominant finger marks on a delicate piece look like blemishes imposed from without. Imagine a magnolia petal with arbitrary dents all over it! Some delicate dimples do stay to speak of the way in which the pot was formed, and make extra-translucent little patches. Although the pieces are very fragile when dry, I have to scrape them at this stage, because a piece which is even slightly damp is a little flexible and may crack through being bent. The fragility of porcelain at all stages is another reason why it is exciting to do; it is difficult right up to the end.

On the whole, the size of the pinched forms is determined by the size of your hand, but you can rest bigger pots in a cradle of foam and start again. You really have to have formed the lower part by pinching as much as the length of your thumb will allow before you start attacking the top. Anyway, the ultimate form of the finished pot is decided here, in the base. This is the root, from which the rest grows naturally. I used to make large ceramics, as big as the kiln would take, when I was doing stoneware, but they took up so much space, so much time, so much sheer repetition when made by coiling that I was pleased to get them finished and out of the way. I really prefer things that you are able to hold and appreciate in your hands, turning them easily around. Made entirely in the hands, without any machinery such as a wheel, they inevitably have a tactile quality, a hand-held shape.

Every now and then, usually following one period of concentrated work, and preceding the next, I change and add to the 'gallery' of pictures which cover the walls of my studio. These are mostly photographs of natural forms, reminders of various qualities which it may be possible to translate into terms of clay and glaze. They are important to me, and having them all around helps me when starting a new series of pots. So do my boxes and shelves of collections of pebbles, shells, twigs and pods. They are a guide to the sorts of thing that happen in nature. I keep them in groups of similar structures with individual differences. When I am working and feel that something is wrong with a piece, it is usually because it would not actually happen that way in nature. It must look like a possible natural form—but not a copy of an existing one.

My pen sketches are a method of noting ideas. They used to be more detailed, and I really wish that I had more time to do careful, probing drawings still. Probably I am thinking more in clay, now that I am more familiar with its potential, and often I do tiny sketches in the clay itself of things which I hope to develop. They are three-dimensional notes which I hope to go back to.

So many ideas come to mind, which I do not get time to explore fully. Sometimes I manage to do only two or three examples before moving on to the next idea. The latest idea is always the stimulating one, each piece out of the kiln suggests exciting expansions of a theme. Even if you want to stand

Conical Veined Bowl (1975), Dappled Bowl (1976) and Interlocking Speckle (1975). All pinched in porcelain and painted with coloured oxides.

still, or go back to old enthusiasms, you cannot always do so, because the work itself actually pushes you, and you are not necessarily in control of the direction in which things are going—you have to do what is honestly interesting you at the moment. You need to find ways of discipling yourself when you work alone. For example, there are times when I would rather do the gardening during the day, which means working in the studio until past two in the morning and getting up very early. But when work is going well you are able to find enormous energy. An exhibition is something for which you have to do your best work by a certain date, and that acts as a stimulus.

I don't think there has been much change in my approach since I first started potting. The main differences are in being able to make things successfully more often, not having so many failures, having a larger range of materials that I have experimented with, more glazes that I know. For about the first four years all my stoneware was unglazed. I rubbed in oxides or raw ash, painted with coloured slips, added oxides to the clay itself which coloured it right through, giving a stone-like quality. I experimented for three years before I managed to make the black glaze I was looking for— the first glaze I used—putting a sample into every kiln which I fired. I wanted something that was matt, not too glossy, not too runny, yet had a slight shine that highlighted the form.

I use more colour now. In nature, colour enhances and defines forms and sometimes makes them blend into their surroundings. I am fascinated by speckled and dappled things—the speckling on trout, the inside of flowers, birds' eggs and broken shadows on water. I use a mixture of oxides painted on in a sort of pointillist way to give variations in depth and to mix the colours. The colouring of the porcelain is done on the raw clay. I have now evolved a great many colours and glazes in which I am able to interpret new ideas. When I first started I found it frustrating to sketch and have an idea, but to be unable to make it materialize. You have to gain the knowledge slowly by working, and be very patient with yourself.

I keep exhaustive notes. I have notes of every pot I have ever made, of each kiln firing and every glaze experiment, because it would be absolutely infuriating to take something from the kiln and be unable to repeat the qualities. There are so many permutations—the firing temperature, whether it was soaked at the end, how high the biscuit temperature was, or even whether there was a little bit of another oxide on the saucer which I hadn't bothered to wash before starting to paint the clay. All of these add up, and if you get something absolutely marvellous and unexpected, say on a corner, you are able to look for something similar in the notes from maybe years back, and possibly come to some conclusion which will enable you to do it on purpose next time. There is always something to learn, and new experiments to be made. That, and the actual satisfaction of handling the clay make it all completely absorbing.

Speckled Egg.

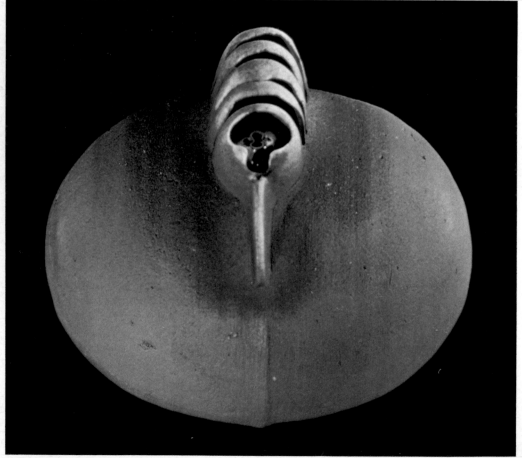

Peter Starkey

Peter Starkey, after finishing the potters' course at Harrow School of Art, ran his own pottery at Hunworth in Norfolk. With his wife Frances and a part-time assistant, he produced domestic ware and some individual pieces in stoneware and porcelain, all salt glazed. Since Autumn 1975, he has been working on the establishment of the Dartington Hall pottery, of which he is manager and a director.

I choose to work in salt glaze because I am greatly attracted to the richness of textures, the colours, the excitement of the firing, the uncertainty of the result, and the immediacy with which the pot 'comes over' to the viewer. With conventional glazing, the pot has to be covered in a coat of glaze, as a kind of skin, which can, and often does, pose problems in relating the glaze and the body. Only when integration is complete does the pot, for me anyway, become a totally satisfying object. In the salting process, the surface of the pot melts to form a glaze, thereby giving an integrated whole. For me, this is very important.

I enjoy the making process very much—the physical contact with the clay, in throwing, turning, handling, cutting or incising. I like to feel the object grow and develop, wondering from stage to stage how it will ultimately look. I am making decisions, sometimes after long deliberation, sometimes spontaneously, sensing something happening between the various elements of the pot, and hoping to achieve a rightness of proportion.

There is one principal respect in which salting helps me to produce in pots the kind of 'feel' I want. Although glazing inevitably covers the surface of the clay, hiding it in some part, salting does the opposite; it reveals and emphasizes the surface, like water on a piece of dull stone. This means that the marks left on the clay by the making process are exaggerated, the evidence of making exposed. Since I enjoy decorating pots in the soft or leather hard stage, this suits me very well. I deliberately make or decorate pots with built in features such as beading, combing, or ridging, upon which I hope the salt will produce interesting effects.

Basically, the salting process works through the interaction between clay and salt vapour at a temperature of around 1260°C. All clays contain silica, which is a glass former and becomes chemically reactive as the body matures. When the temperature reaches 1270°C, damp salt is thrown into the kiln at intervals. This causes a chemical reaction between the sodium

Top. PETER STARKEY. Salt glazed bowl.
Bottom. GEOFFREY SWINDELL. Helmet form with iron oxide and wood ash glaze.

in the resulting salt vapour and the silica in the clay. The silica is attacked by the sodium and melts, thus forming the coat of glaze on the pot. Obviously the amount of glaze depends on the silica content of the clay—the more silica, the smoother and more brilliant the resulting surface. In clays containing less silica, a more broken, mottled texture results, as the sodium seeks out particles of silica with which to combine. This naturally means that the type of clay is of paramount importance to the saltglazer. By the use of slips of various clays, a very wide range of textures can be achieved on one pot, from absolute mattness to a brilliant shine.

The potter inevitably has less control over salt glazing than he has when using more conventional methods. The glazing is achieved by a vapour passing through the pots, and as clouds cannot be harnessed, he stands outside the kiln, hoping that each pot is receiving the necessary quota. However, as the kiln is at 1270°C there is nothing he can do but hope that the setting of the kiln was right, and the correct amount of salt is being introduced. Too little and the surface will remain dull, too much and the result will be an unpleasant greenish grey, closely resembling cold porridge. It is a tantalizing situation, and a very exciting one. Instinct plays a big part, as does experience of your kiln. One thing is certain, the results are very seldom predictable, and once they become so they rapidly lose their interest. The very individuality of each pot is for me what it is all about. No two pots are exactly alike, each has received its mark from the vapour and the flame. Every kiln produces its treasures and its disasters, new standards are attained or new problems created.

This undoubtedly makes for economic problems. What is a new achievement or breakthrough to me as a salt glazer is meaningless to a layman or even a fellow potter. What price another colour not yet achieved till now? It excites me, but what value do I put on it? The 'seconds' rate is often high —salting is a capricious medium, but then, that is its attraction. I cannot

Lidded boxes in salt glazed porcelain, decorated with coloured slips, and (right) storage jar in stoneware with incised decoration.

have it all ways. I have to take the good luck with the bad and try to learn from each firing.

I strongly believe that aesthetics and the making process cannot be divided. Aesthetic development often emanates from a purely technical breakthrough (as was the case when the art of porcelain was rediscovered in eighteenth-century Europe). When one is involved in making anything, how and why become almost impossible to separate. I came to use clay as I do by a process of elimination, trying other materials—paint, wood, metal, stone etc.—and making functional and non-functional objects. I found that clay suited me best. It enabled me to explore ideas rapidly, as the making process is swift and infinitely versatile. The sensibilities which I hope I exercised in other disciplines, for example sculptural considerations of mass and space,

and qualities associated with drawing—colour, tonal and textural relation-ships—are equally employed in clay. Also, with potting, the processes are infinitely seductive and very satisfying in themselves.

Most of my work is functional at the moment. In addition to my enjoy-ment of the making, I get a great kick out of using something I have made and finding that it works on a purely functional level. Obviously the question must arise whether the necessary restrictions of concept dictated by function militate too strongly against freedom of expression. I would argue that they do not. The sensibilities employed in making objects for use or for their own sake are not that different. Plastic and other qualities unite them both. Each is a vehicle of communication, one through use, the other by the individual's response to the form. To me, a use is a bonus, not an excuse for a lack of conceptual capacity. However, people cannot fail to wonder, when perfectly functional pots are being produced by industry, if it is not anachronistic to be making them by hand, far less efficiently and often expensively. What sort of alternative does it really offer a potential pur-chaser? Is the maker simply some quirky flat-earther who refuses to relate to the reality of modern life, or can his use of a seventeenth-century tech-nique really make any contribution, however small, to improving the quality of his own life or that of his customers? I must of course maintain that it can. I believe that industrial pots are often bereft of humanity and totally lacking in communication between maker and user. 'So what?' asks the layman, 'I just want something to drink tea from.' He may be right, who can say?

Nevertheless, I find it heartening that many people are reacting today against the debilitating effects of mass production and are seeking alter-native, more personal life styles through which they can dictate their own standards and exercise genuine choices—just be individuals. Being a studio potter is, I suppose, such a choice, and enough people seem to be in sym-pathy with what I make to give me a living. I hope this is a vote of con-fidence.

I do enjoy what I do, and I think that aspect is infinitely important. The delight in what you do comes over in your work; you have to care for your pots. Often the pressures of survival can depress. This is a constant problem, and we either solve it in our different ways, or compromise our basic feelings about our work.

The dialogue between a potter and his work never ceases. The method of making is a continually enlivening factor. The pot grows in stages, the clay changes from plastic to dry, is then fired and glazed, at each stage giving back messages which must be assimilated and acted upon. In salting, the transformation from raw pot to glazed is so drastic, so much to do with the fire and not me, that I regard the pots as objects completely in their own right, to be cherished or despised on their own merits.

Large storage jar in salt glazed stoneware.

Salt glazed stoneware plate with impressed decoration.

The firing is a great maker or undoer. However much work has been done on them before, the pots have to be risked in the kiln. Fortunately I enjoy firing as much as making; with salting it is just as creative, not merely an uneventful finishing process to be gone through with the minimum fuss and the maximum predictability. Fire really excites me. As a child, I was always in trouble for lighting fires; now I can indulge myself entirely. All the elements of drama are there: the slow build up of heat, influencing the flame patterns until the right temperature is reached, a dramatic finale when the salt is introduced, with the resulting flames, smoke and fumes (shades of Frankenstein!) Then, the wait until the kiln is cool enough to open. Anticipation is everything. In my mind's eye, I have a vision of the pots, and although the result usually falls far short of my expectations, occasionally a pot emerges that is far above my hopes. When I unpack a kiln, I always have a terrific urge to fill it up again quickly, either to rectify mistakes or to repeat and improve upon successes. I am an incurable optimist, firmly convinced that the next firing will be terrific. Making pots is a continually satisfying life; I hope mine convey to other people some of the enjoyment I had in making them.

Salt glazed stoneware plate with incised decoration.

Geoffrey Swindell

Geoffrey Swindell builds objects from a combination of freehand modelling and press moulding in porcelain and occasionally stoneware. He has recently been doing some work in association with woodworker Steve Grant, who has created settings for the pots. He is a lecturer at Cardiff School of Art.

I did purely functional pottery for about a year when I was a student in Stoke. After spending five years as a painting student, I had a fairly good background in painting and I felt that I wanted to do something original with ceramics, not the usual treacle toffee stuff that was being produced in colleges at the time. Of course, it is not like that in pottery departments today. I worked in a studio pottery for a short time, and that got me interested—I had originally applied to do a painting course, but I backed out of it at the last moment, stayed in Stoke, where I was born, and did a ceramics course.

My relations nearly all worked in some way in the pottery industry. My mother and grandmother were paintresses, my grandfather stoked the old

Porcelain forms with dolomite glaze, (below) with incised lines, and sand blasted surface.

bottle kilns. My father, as an electrician, is about the only one in the family who was not involved. I do not think that environment was an important influence. I was never interested in industrial design as a student. It is a very bad thing to be a designer in Stoke-on-Trent because it is underpaid and extremely limiting. Few new shapes are produced, and styles are largely controlled by American taste. Since Americans seem to like traditional English pottery, that is all designers get a chance to draw up, and English people buy contemporary work from Scandinavia if they can afford it. My background simply meant that I was brought up with all the terminology of pottery: words like glost firings, biscuit ware and fettling I knew about as a child.

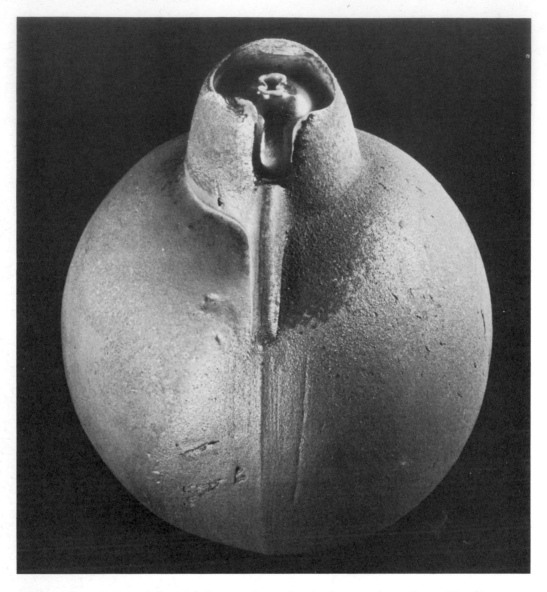

Helmet form in porcelain with iron and wood ash glaze and on-glaze silver lustre.

I spent seven years at Stoke and then three years at the Royal College of Art, where I was taught by Hans Coper. He influenced me a lot, not by his work so much as the attitude expressed in his teaching. I regard him as one of the great originals, one of the best people working this century, because his work owes nothing to anything or anyone at all. The work of Cardew, Leach and potters like them does not really impress me artistically, because it is not original, not creative, not breaking through any stylistic barriers. Their work is just reiterative of old values. I read *A Potter's Book* without actually agreeing with Leach's philosophy. I understood it, certainly; getting away from industrial ware and producing something by hand can be good if someone wants to do it. At the same time, I do not really believe that is a very valid thing to do—the manufacturers make something that is very good to use, and I do not think that the studio potter produces very practical tableware. It is usually rather heavy and scratches surfaces or pulls the tablecloth off. I use old willow pattern made in Stoke.

I started out working exclusively from natural forms. Then, six years ago, I began to collect tin toys. I don't know why—there is no reason at all—I just liked them. At the time, they had nothing to do with my work. Perhaps it was because they were just the opposite. But after two years I suddenly noticed that some of my pots were developing fins, sharp corners, bubbles and cockpits, and I realized that the toys were having an influence. That is how a lot of my ideas are worked out. I do not sit down and think, What can I make? How can I get some ideas? At that stage, I do not work from anything very specific, I simply work from something that's inside. I cannot really explain it at all. I do not know how I get ideas, other than by surrounding myself with things I like, which eventually start to affect my images and work. The tactile side of my work is very important to me, perhaps the small scale makes that inevitable.

In 1974, I got interested in helmets, and they started to appear in the forms. Once I realize that I am being influenced by something, I really do study it thoroughly. I went to Paris to look at the helmets in the military museum, taking a lot of photographs that I could study when I came home. The most obviously helmet-like forms date from early 1974. At the time, they seemed to me much stronger and more interesting than the delicate pink pots. I was more pleased with them, if I am pleased with my work at all; they seemed to be more about what I wanted to make. I do not think I ever wanted to make pots very much and these seem to be further removed than some of the others with fairly open tops. But possibly a lot of people who make pots wouldn't consider anything I ever made a pot at all!

Small porcelain forms (left) with articulated decoration, incised lines filled with copper, dolomite glaze, and (right) with extruded strands of clay, black glaze.

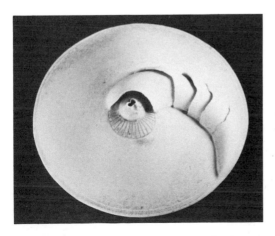 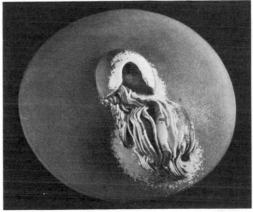

Small, ovoid porcelain form, dolomite glaze coloured with copper, and (opposite) helmet form, porcelain, with iron oxide and wood ash glaze, sand blasted surface.

There is a contrast between the well established potters of the 1950s and 1960s, and the whole group of people who came out of the Royal College around 1969–71, like Jackie Poncelet, Paul Astbury, Glenys Barton, Elizabeth Fritsch, who are now forming the 'establishment' of the 1970s and seem to me much more creative, a group of artists rather than craftsmen and potters; that's the main difference really. They have an elaborate approach to their work, probably much less humble, more self-conscious, than the older potters. People are usually surprised when they come here and see me at home—I think they expect something more like a potter, the sandals, chunky sweater, beard and natural food image. I do not live the rustic life that many potters seem to enjoy.

Most of us in the younger group have some sort of outside stimulus that we start from and bring into our work. My own stimuli arise from fish and other sea forms, toys and miniaturised objects, which seem in my later work to be coming closer together. On the other hand, a lot of the older potters seem to have this mania for clay and glazes. I couldn't care less about that, and I am certainly not the type to grind my own materials. I'll buy them— I don't want to mess about, it's the idea that matters, the end result. I

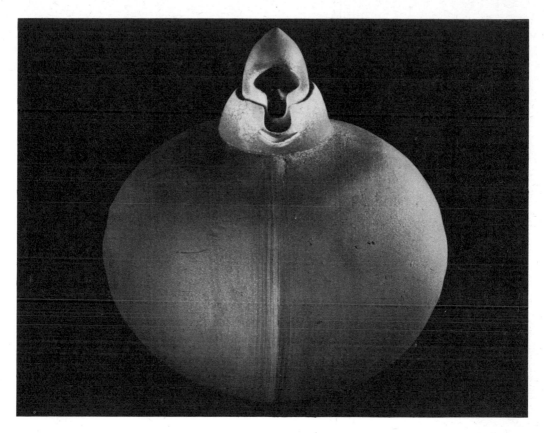

would derive no satisfaction from finding materials or building a kiln. In fact, I know very little about it. That is another great difference: most of the young people are really not concerned with that do-it-all-yourself stuff, maybe because life has been easier for them, and materials and equipment are readily available. Until 1960 it was difficult to get any materials or any equipment unless you built it yourself. I think standards have risen, too. You see, before the war, if you could throw a pot on a wheel you were quite something, whereas I have had amateur students produce better work in evening classes than some of the people who became well known for their throwing then.

Some people seem rather nervous about this younger group, but of course behind us there is yet another lot coming along with more 'fine art' ideas—out of wheel-made pottery altogether. Many students, curiously enough, are making very literal objects, rather like a lot of the replica pottery in my collection, thinking they are doing something very new. Actually, they are working in a very old western tradition, but one that is completely different from the traditions of the Sung dynasty. Their rather literal approach seems to me to be bringing ceramics nearer to the world of fine art, though I do not think that the fine art world is yet very interested.

The ceramics world is always in this difficult situation, where people hope to be taken seriously and want their prices to go up in line with sculpture and painting. Of course, they won't, because very rarely is anyone making a creative or progressive statement in clay that is good enough to be taken on the same sort of level as David Hockney, Henry Moore or any other well-known artist of our time. It is possible for the individual artist to reach some very high standard—I think someone like Hans Coper has. But the prices are so different. Hans Coper sells a pot for well under £100, which is nothing, and he is, let's say, the Henry Moore of the ceramic world. But, unlike Moore, he does not make a fortune out of it.

I do believe in some truth to material. I make things which, I hope, speak about clay, fire and glaze to some extent. I do not see any point in producing in clay something that you could make more easily in plastic, fibre glass, or anything else. When clay is wet it is very easily modelled, and to make objects that are somehow fluid seems to accept the properties of the material. You are fantastically limited in what you can do.

I have a personality with many contradictions. I make very quiet, introspective work and yet I play the drums as hard as I can hit them, rock 'n' roll style, and that is actually what I enjoy much more than making ceramics. When I was a painter, I used a lot of physical energy. I used to paint on the floor becuase I'ld knock the easels over and I couldn't use canvas because I'd rip through it with my palette knife. Yet when I became a potter, this other side of my character emerged—I don't know why. My ceramics are nothing to do with emotional outburst. They seem to be very controlled and thoughtful, very cool. Even so, I do not usually work a thing out before I make it. I make the plaster moulds from a collection of all sorts of odds and ends, plastic bananas, parts of aircraft kits, buttons, pen tops—anything—and then I assemble them to see if the arrangement works. If it doesn't, I try another and slowly build up a form. If I like the result, I'll repeat it and improve it about half a dozen times, pick out the best and keep that myself. Most of the others will be scrapped, and one or two I will sell. I find I use that potter's approach of repetition sometimes. It is a good thing to repeat successful forms and sometimes, if I haven't got any ideas, I make something I have done before, just for the sake of working, for the discipline. And then some new idea will come along, usually by accident.

What I am looking for at the moment is a cross between organic forms and man-made forms. You find that, say, a speed boat and a fish are very closely related in structure, and I am trying to make an object now that achieves a synthesis of the two things without giving the immediate impression of a fish or a speed boat. I want people who look at them not really to know what they are, or what my stimulus comes from. I am not aiming at anything that literally looks like a boat or a fish. I do not know much about the mechanics—it's just a visual thing that matters to me.

Just as I do not mix my own materials, I know very little about the theory of glazing, apart from what I have done myself. I would be unable

Helmet form. Porcelain form, sand blasted. Miniature form on stoneware base.

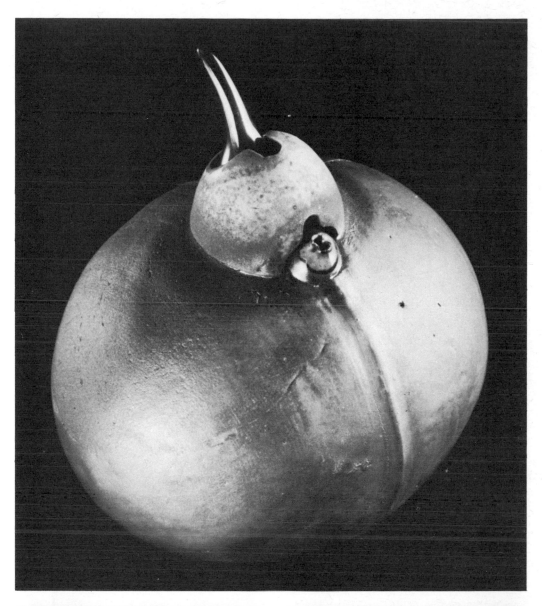

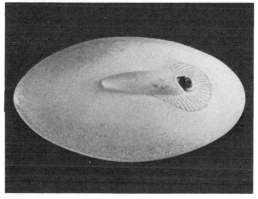
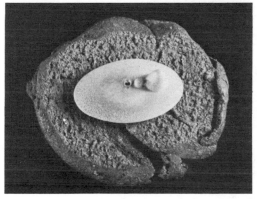

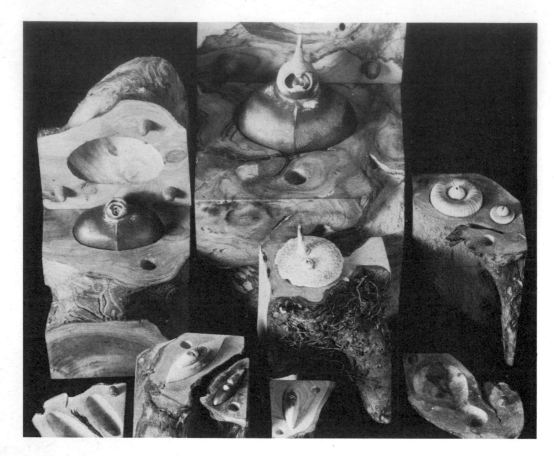

to talk to anyone about glazing, or lecture on it. I do not think you have to know the chemical formulae. I simple experiment empirically. Derek Emms, who was taught by Leach and knew a lot about the technicalities gave me some recipes when I was a student in Stoke, and I change or adapt as I need them simply by adding a shake of this and a spoonful of that. If it works, it works, and if not, I take some away and try some other ingredient. The glazes have been built up by trial and error, not by any real knowledge. One, for instance, is not a glaze, it's absolutely dry, I wanted it dry, I like it. I could make it shiny if I wanted to, but if you took it to a chemist who was not in any way an artist he would say that it did not work—but a glaze is for decorative effect, not for any functional purpose, except in earthenware.

Sometimes I use a sand blaster, the kind of thing they clean buildings with. Mine is in a hood container, with a face plate you can see through. You put your hands inside big rubber gloves, to use it, so that it is very difficult to hold on to the ceramics, especially as I am hitting the form with 80 pounds per square inch of air and sand. You cannot really see what you are doing, there is too much dust. I have no real control over it. Sometimes, I go right through the pot, or simply do not achieve the right result. I cannot help losing a few at that stage because the machine is so powerful. I use it when the pot is completely finished and glazed, getting that very dry, pitted texture by blasting off the glaze. There was a blaster in the glass department at the Royal College, and Hans Coper once suggested that I go and use it when I had a glaze I did not like. That was the first I had ever heard of it. I went up and sand blasted, thought it had fantastic potential, rushed back for a whole load of other things, and ruined them completely because they just had not needed blasting.

I had great trouble with dunting (cracking on cooling) at one time. My ceramics are so thin that the glaze, if I apply it only to the outside, is almost as thick as the body. The glaze and body need to have the same rate of contraction as they cool. If the two are not compatible, they draw apart. But if you glaze the inside as well, the whole thing seems to hold together. I had to find a way of glazing the inside, which was becoming more and more difficult as the holes in the tops of the pots were growing smaller. I got round the problem by squeezing a certain amount of the glaze in with a syringe, shaking it, and pouring out the excess. Then I wipe and spray the outside. I do not think it is a difficulty many other potters would suffer from very much. I still get other problems with warping and twisting.

I work in a very light-coloured stoneware and porcelain. Since I was a student, I have never made anything in earthenware. I do not like the feel of it—when it is finished, it is too soft, too fragile. Porcelain is difficult to work with, feels like putty; it collapses, dries quickly and has no plasticity.

Small porcelain forms in wooden setting made by Steve Grant. Column structures in white porcelain, hand built with moulded details, some brightly enamelled.

GEOFFREY SWINDELL

I have made some porcelain pastes in the past, but I buy it now. Most of the proprietary brands are much better, anyway, but you sometimes need to mix them for the result you want. I try to keep clay for a year before I use it; most kinds improve with age. I think many potters enjoy preparing their own materials—my attitude is not typical at all. But I do not live like that, I have not got time. Teaching and just generally living, washing clothes, shopping, going out for a drink, or driving to the coast are time consuming. I'ld say I worked on my own ceramics two days a week on average, more if I feel the need.

I enjoy teaching, it is creative and brings me into contact with a lot of people. It also gives me time to work if I want to. In any case, I haven't enough creative power to work seven days a week. It would mean too much repetition to make a living. I repeat to a certain extent now, merely because I need to get things right, but how can you go on producing something new every day? I do not run a business and I do not take commissions or anything like that for money. I would be working as a craftsman, doing a simple job of craftsmanship rather than trying to be creative. I make what I want to make. If people want it they buy it and if not they don't. It does not matter, because I live on my lecturer's pay and that is the way I prefer it.

I know that if I run out of ideas and go on being unable to produce anything new, I shall retire, finish, I could not go on. I will not stop teaching ceramics, I enjoy doing that, I shall simply stop working in ceramics and go on to something else. I might go back to painting or turn more seriously to photography, which I have been interested in for a long time but have never really been able to get at because my pots have taken up all the time. But I have no intention of simply repeating forever—the sort of thing that potters do, of course. Once they have a line, it is almost like a good gimmick, and they just go on producing it. Though there have been a number of times when I have thought I was finished and had no more ideas left, was burned out, in fact, some accident has happened to give me a new idea and, so far, the work has not stopped developing.

I do not think there are any rules about what pots should be like. Too many people make up rules, like the only thing you can do with clay is put it on a potter's wheel. Well I do not agree. Some time ago, I did an exhibition and lectures at Sutton College in Surrey, showing eight years' work. It was mainly intended for amateur potters. I wanted to try and explain how I arrived at my present work from my start eight years before in clay. It is a big problem to convey to amateurs, who go away and make pots like pots they have seen before, that there is something else involved, that a potter can work as creatively as a painter. People often look at my work and fail to understand what it does. Is it a salt cellar or a cigarette lighter? They don't know what it's for, which always annoys me because they don't expect a painting or sculpture to have any specific function like that.

Column structures, hand built and moulded; details with on-glaze lustre.

Yeap Poh Chap

Yeap Poh Chap works at his own pottery in Surrey in the traditions of Chinese ceramics. He recreates on stoneware and porcelain some of the glazes and effects developed in China from the Sung dynasty: celadon, crackle glazes, peachbloom, tenmoku and brush painting.

I became a potter very late in life, and was a useless human being until I discovered clay about fourteen years ago. I was in Denmark visiting my wife's parents, who work very hard and were terribly upset when they found that I was not doing any work. When I had to renew my visa after three months, the immigration people refused to let me stay any longer because I had no job, although I could keep myself and had guarantors that I would not be a burden on the Danish economy. I was not allowed to accept a job I had been offered, simply because it was one that a Dane could do. I agreed entirely. Back home I went, thinking that the situation was hopeless and I would have to come back to London. But my wife's father, who was a bank manager, had once helped a potter to start and took me round to see if I could be used in the pottery. The potter agreed, out of gratitude to the bank manager, I'm sure, and I was taken on as the odd job man.

Small bowl thrown and shaped in stoneware; celadon glaze with iron brushwork.

Porcelain bowl with ice coloured crackle glaze.

I did everything. It was the first time I had seen clay in my life. My family had never had any connection with the arts, they were all in business. I was paid one-and-six an hour, working eight or ten hours a day, for all the heavy work, like carting clay, and all the dirty jobs that nobody wanted to do. I'm glad I did all that because it's always good to start from the beginning. While there, I kept my eyes open, I watched the potters, did a bit of decorating under supervision and, towards the end, I was given a few hints on how to throw.

I stuck it out for six months before coming back to London. Because I had never had any art training, I didn't dare approach any art school. Mind you, I was in my thirties. If I had been nineteen, I would have barged into any art school, but at my age I didn't dare. I joined the pottery class at an evening institute in Putney and treated it as an art school. I was the first in and the last out every day, five days a week. I even asked for permission to work during the weekends. I was turned down, 'We don't do that.' Then

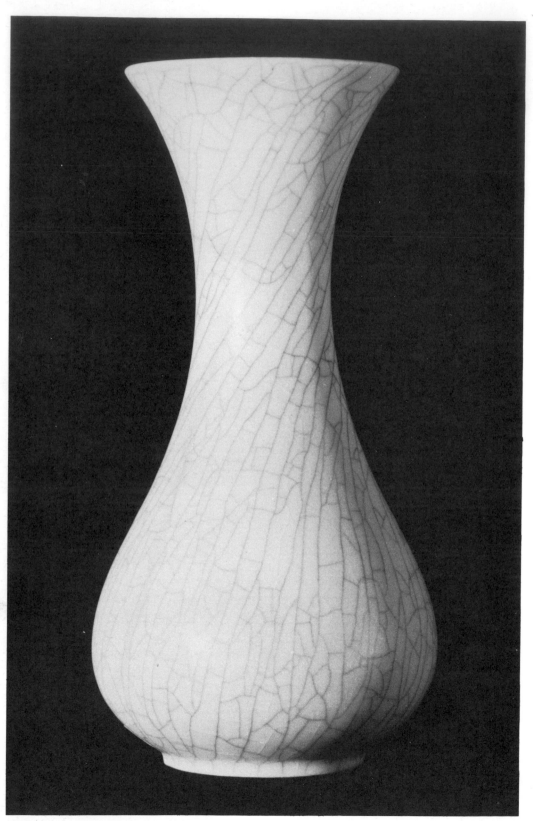

Porcelain vase, white glaze with Chinese ink rubbed in crackle; stoneware teapot, fluted sides, with dark brown tenmoku glaze.

one of the instructors said, 'Look, I don't think there's anything much we can do to help you further. Would you like to go to an art school?' I said I would be very grateful if they could fix it for me, and an appointment was made at the Hammersmith College of Art. I went there with some work and was accepted as a full time student.

It was very hard work. I felt I had no time to play around. I had to decide what kind of pottery to do. It is a very wide field, and I had to restrict myself to the style I had chosen. For that reason, I concentrated on my own work and nothing else. I had a lot of problems with the authorities in the school, simply because I refused to draw or to do anything else. I had to explain to them that at my age I had no time to muck around and I knew what kind of pottery I wanted to do. I had proved I was prepared to work hard, they could see that. I was responsible, and I knew what I wanted to do. After I had convinced them, I had no more problems. I fired

the kiln as often as I could, even for other students, simply because I feel, even now, that a potter without a knowledge of fire is not a complete potter. If he doesn't know fire, there's no point. It's just not good enough to have to depend on another potter if you want to be a professional. And so I fired at least one or two kilns a week.

After the first year, the students had to put up a show of sorts, and an instructor from the Royal College came and looked at my work. We had a chat, he liked some things, not others, and nothing more. The following weekend, I met the same instructor by chance in a pub not far from where I was living. I grumbled that I had three months on my hands with nothing to do and no place to work. He said he would see what he could do. A few days later, I had a card saying, 'Permission has been obtained for you to work at the Royal College during the vacation.' I flew there, of course, to thank David Queensberry for allowing me to work there and promised not

Stoneware dishes with sponged decoration and (above) prawn design in iron pigment.

to get in anybody's way. Then I worked there for three months, and I did the same thing for three years. When the other students were having their holidays, I was working. Not only that, I sold a lot of work at varying prices.

Towards the end of my third year at Hammersmith, David Queensberry gave me an offer, which I gratefully accepted, to do research. So I started officially as a research student in 1967. Ian Godfrey and I were the first two to take advantage of a scheme whereby two so-called established potters could do research at the Royal College for a year. Since then, it has been extended to two years, but we only did one.

I had taken pots round in a suitcase as a student, but I am one of the few potters who did not have to go through the usual channels of little exhibitions in craft shops and things like that, where prices are not commensurate

Porcelain stem cup with pale crackle glaze. Stoneware bottle, glaze flecked with iron.

with the hard work put in by potters—I am not talking purely about myself, but most potters. During the private view of my first exhibition at the Brian Koetser fine art gallery, in 1973, I sold £2,000 worth of pottery. How I got there was pure luck, nothing more, nothing less. One day, a woman rang up to ask if she could come and look at my pottery and my work. Well, I said, 'Of course you may, welcome, come round and have a look, the pottery is very small.' She bought a pot and then asked if I would have a look at her work—she is an amateur potter. Warned that I would say only what I felt to be the truth, she said she was prepared for it and showed me one of her pots. The body was alright, but the lid was a bit truncated so, with her permission, I added some clay, which made it more agreeable to my eyes, and she was delighted. A few days later, she brought her husband, a collector of Chinese antiques, to look at my work. They bought some pots and said they would like to come back some other time. Then they rang up and asked if I wanted an exhibition, just out of the blue. They arranged for me to visit the gallery with some work, which was accepted for an exhibition. It was as simple as that.

I set myself very strict standards. When I was learning to throw, for instance, I drove myself very hard. I do feel that a craftsman needs integrity.

Nothing less than a hundred per cent integrity will do. In other words, I would like to be able to say I have no sentiments. My reason for saying such a thing is this: for me, a bad pot is a bad pot, regardless, and I cannot make excuses. I cannot say that it is a bad day, or my stomach is not quite right. It's always *mea culpa*, I'm not good enough—no excuses, ever. I have to throw out pots I don't like. I want to be a professional, you see. I am, in a way, and I'm a very ambitious potter. Why waste my time? I have to seek perfection in my work—no lies, no bluffs, no gimmicks.

Because Chinese pottery is so much admired, it sets standards which a lot of potters try to achieve. Bowls that one sees done by potters everywhere are essentially based on Chinese or Japanese bowls. But Japanese bowls have always been based on Chinese bowls, and so . . . I feel very strongly that if I were to make any other kind of pot, I would be bogus. After all, I have a cultural heritage I can be very proud of. In the field of pottery, no other country or people can equal the work that my ancestors have turned out and, for this reason, what better source can I search for? I used to go often to museums, to devour books and magazines and train myself to look. Although my inspiration comes from Chinese pottery, I like to think that I have managed to inject my own personality. My bowls are based on traditional shapes, but I hope they are unmistakably mine.

Although I am Chinese, I have never been to China, nor has my father, nor my grandfather. We have been in Malaya for quite a few generations, longer than some Malayans. However, I would like to go, purely for sentimental reasons, because it is the source of all my culture, just as Australians, New Zealanders and Americans come to visit Britain. I should like to go and see the potteries. The Japanese have done a lot of work on promoting their own potteries, but the Chinese have never bothered really.

The ancient Chinese felt that the reason for making a pot is first of all its function. A pot without function is something that never occurred to them, I think. And then they maintain that a pot performing a function, whatever it is, can also be a thing of beauty. That is the reasoning behind it. I try to work with this axiom in mind. You could say, I suppose, that a decorative pot performs a function, but that would not be quite honest—it appears hypocritical to me. That flower vase is a simple faceted cylinder. It was meant to be a vase, and I would say that it performs a useful function. It is an honest pot.

I feel that a potter must pot. If he strives to be as good at it as he can, he fulfils all the function that is necessary in a potter. A painter must paint, a potter must pot—and do so with complete integrity and honesty. To get anywhere, he must have ideals, he must have a standard. Let others decide, let others interpret. His job as a human being is done. I have something against being bogus, being dishonest. It would be terrible for a potter, for me, to interpret. I love to say to people, especially people dealing with design, do anything you like, make it work. Now, having achieved that, simplify it. Simplicity, that is what I strive for in my work.

Biographies

ALAN BARRETT-DANES

Born 1936 in Kent. Family connected with potteries at Hoo, Rainham and Upchurch. Studied at colleges of art in Maidstone and Stoke-on-Trent. Worked as a designer in the pottery industry in Stoke-on-Trent, where he also taught part-time; subsequently lecturer at Nuneaton School of Art and Slough Technical College. Now Senior Lecturer in Ceramics at Cardiff College of Art. Early work mainly wheel-thrown; since 1972, has made individual pieces, from 1974 in collaboration with wife, Ruth, who originally trained as illustrator. Exhibitions include one man show at Keele University; 'International Ceramics', Victoria & Albert Museum, London (1972); 'New Directions in Ceramics', Oxford Gallery, 'Craftsman's Art', Victoria & Albert Museum, London, 'Earth and Fire', Welsh Arts Council (1973); International Exhibition of Ceramic Art, Chunichi, Japan, 'Towards Ceramic Sculpture', Oxford Gallery, 'New Ceramics', British Crafts Centre (1974); Contemporary English Ceramics, Kilkenny, Eire, International Ceramics Symposium, National Museum of Wales (1975); 'Seven in '76', Portsmouth Museum (1976).

SVEND BAYER

Born 1946 in East Africa of Danish parents. Studied Geography and Economics at University of Exeter. Worked for Michael Cardew at Wenford Bridge Pottery (1969–72) and then for five months at a pottery in Barnstaple, North Devon. After travelling in the Far East, returned to Wenford Bridge (October 1973–late January 1974); subsequently worked in America with Todd Piker. In 1975, established own pottery at Sheepwash, North Devon. Work shown at Kettle's Yard, Cambridge (1974) and Craftsman Potters' Shop (1975).

ALAN CAIGER-SMITH

Born 1930. Studied at Camberwell School of Art & Crafts (1948–49), and at King's College, Cambridge (1949–52). Studied pottery at Central School of Art & Design in 1954, then established Aldermaston Pottery (1955). Book,

Tin-Glaze Pottery in Europe and the Islamic World, published (1973) by Faber & Faber, London. First exhibition at Heal's in London (1958); work shown since in Japan and Australia, and at Faenza. Work in public collections, including Victoria & Albert Museum, National Museum of Wales, (St Fagans), Paisley Museum, Reading Museum & Art Gallery, Curtis Museum, Alton (Hants), County Education Authority collections, Abbot Hall Art Gallery, Kendal (Cumbria), Hanover Museum, National Museum, Faenza, Australian National University Collection, National Gallery of Victoria, Australia, Boymans van Beuningen Museum, Rotterdam.

MICHAEL CARDEW

Born 1901. Learned to throw with William Fishley Holland at Fremington, North Devon. In 1923, went to work at St Ives pottery as Bernard Leach's first pupil. In 1926, reopened Winchcombe Pottery, Gloucestershire, where production of flower pots and domestic ware had ceased in 1915; made lead-glazed earthenware with slip trailed, combed or sgraffito decoration; exhibited at Royal Institute Galleries (1931). Established pottery at Wenford Bridge, near Bodmin, Cornwall, in 1939, later returning to work at Winchcombe for a short time. In 1942, took over from Harry Davis for three years as pottery instructor at Achimota College, Gold Coast (now Ghana). Subsequently, built pottery and started stoneware production at Vumé-Dugamé, Gold Coast. Again at Wenford Bridge in 1948, turned over production to stoneware. As Pottery Officer to Nigerian Government (1950–65), set up pottery training centre at Abuja, Northern Nigeria in 1951, teaching native potters to make stoneware thrown on wheel. In 1968, went to Australia to help Ivan McMeekin to start pottery for aborigines in Northern Territories. Book, *Pioneer Pottery*, published in Britain (1969) by Longmans and in America by St Martin's Press. Recent exhibitions include Cardew & Associates at Craftsman Potters' Shop (1975) and retrospective at Boymans van Beuningen, Rotterdam (1976).

BIOGRAPHIES

MICHAEL CASSON

Born 1925. Trained as painter; after some teaching, studied pottery at Hornsey School of Art. Subsequently established workshop in London with his wife, Sheila; moved to Great Missenden, Buckinghamshire, in 1959. With Victor Margrie, started vocational course for potters at Harrow School of Art (1963); resumed full time work as potter in 1973. Chairman of the council of Craftsman Potters' Association (1965–67). Book, *Pottery in Britain Today*, published (1967) by Alec Tiranti, London. Recent exhibitions include one man show at British Crafts Centre (1972); 'The Craftsman's Art', Victoria & Albert Museum, London (1973); exhibitions of 100 jugs at Craftwork, Guildford, and of bowls at the Casson Gallery, London (1975).

ELIZABETH FRITSCH

Born 1940 in Wales. Studied harp and piano at Birmingham School of Music from 1960, then studied harp under Osian Ellis at Royal Academy of Music, London (1966). After postgraduate course in ceramics at Royal College of Art (from 1968), spent a year (1972) in Copenhagen, Denmark. Now living in Welwyn Garden City, Hertfordshire. Exhibitions include one man show at Bing & Grøndahl factory, Copenhagen (1972); exhibition at Design Centre, 'Everyman a Patron' at Crafts Advisory Council, 'Towards Ceramic Sculpture' at Oxford Gallery, one man show at Crafts Advisory Council, 'Ceramic Forms', Crafts Advisory Council jointly with British Council (1974).

IAN GODFREY

Born 1941 in London. Studied at first as painter, at Camberwell School of Art & Crafts (1957–62), setting up shared workshop in City Road, Islington, in 1959. In 1962, started teaching one day a week at Camberwell. 1967–68: research fellowship at Royal College of Art. Established workshop in Goswell Road, Islington, in 1968. Began teaching part time at Bristol in 1969. Given a one man show at Primavera by Henry Rothschild (1964); took part in two exhibitions at Quantas Gallery, London, in 1967, a second show at Primavera (1968), and a one man exhibition at the Craft Centre (1974); also exhibited work in Japan. Winner of Gold Medal at International Exhibition of Ceramics, Faenza (1974). Received Crafts Advisory Committee bursary for potters (1975) and has

spent the year mainly in painting and development of experiments in glass. Exhibition of pottery at Heals, London (1976).

MO JUPP

Born 1938. Studied at Camberwell School of Art & Crafts (1960–64) and Royal College of Art (1964–67). Has taught at Medway, Hornsey and Hendon colleges of art; now teaches at Harrow College of Technology & Art and West Surrey College of Art & Design, Farnham. Exhibited in Jugoslavia (1968), Japan (1969), USA (1970), as well as contributing to travelling exhibitions in Britain and Europe. One man shows at Grabowski Gallery (1969) and Craft Centre, London (1972). Contributor to 'Towards Ceramic Sculpture' at Oxford Gallery (1974) and 'Bodybox' at Victoria & Albert Museum (1975).

DAVID LEACH

Born 1910. Joined pottery at St Ives (1930) as apprentice to his father, Bernard Leach. Taught at Dartington Hall School and started pottery there (1933–34). Studied at North Staffordshire Technical College from 1934, receiving Hons. Diploma in 1937; subsequently returned to run Leach Pottery. Initiated training of local apprentices and, in 1938, started making of repeat range of stoneware. After war service (1941–45), returned to form partnership with father and ran Leach Pottery until start of Lowerdown Pottery in 1956. Work as teacher includes establishment of pottery classes at Penzance school of art; acting head of pottery department at Loughborough College of Art & Design (1953–54); visiting lecturer at several art schools; external assessor to Harrow College of Technology & Art studio pottery course; member of Board of Assessors to Scottish Education department. Foundation member of Crafts Centre of Great Britain; past chairman Craftsman Potters' Association Council; Council member, Devon Guild of Craftsmen; until 1974, ceramics representative on Crafts Advisory Council grants sub-committee. Work in collections of museums in Europe, USA, Australia and New Zealand; chosen for 'Craftsman's Art in Europe' at Victoria & Albert Museum (1973). Gold medallist at International Academy Ceramics Exhibition, 1967. Other recent exhibitions include one man show at Museum of Decorative Art, Copenhagen (1973) and, in 1974, exhibitions in Nottingham and Liverpool.

ROGER MICHELL

Born 1947. Studied at Central School of Art & Design (1962–65) before running his own pottery in St John's Wood, London. Subsequently worked for sculptor, Antony Caro, and as gallery assistant at Serpentine Gallery, Hyde Park (1970). Moved to East Knapton, Yorkshire, with wife, Danka Napiorkowska, in 1971; Lustre Pottery in production from 1972; slip casting unit developed in 1975.

DANKA NAPIORKOWSKA

Born 1946. Studied at Central School until 1968 and then took postgraduate diploma in print making at Chelsea College of Art in 1969. While continuing to teach part-time at Central School and in Wimbledon (1971–75), established pottery at East Knapton with Roger Michell. Their exhibitions include 'The Craftsman's Art', Victoria & Albert Museum (1973), 'International Ceramics', Faenza, Italy (1973); also at C. T. Strangeways, London, Wolverhampton Art Gallery (1974), Cartier, New York, London Design Centre Summer Exhibition (1975).

BRYAN NEWMAN

Born 1935 in London. Took two-year general course at Camberwell Art School, then specialized in pottery under Hugh Purdy and Dick Kendal. A year later, returned to Camberwell as technical assistant and part-time teacher. Also taught at Bath Academy and Harrow School of Art. In 1961, established studio with three other potters in London; moved to Somerset (1966). Since first exhibition with Ian Auld at Primavera, London, in 1960, has had several one and two man exhibitions, and taken part in many group shows. Work shown in Tokyo, Copenhagen, Sydney and Munich, and in collections of Inner London Education Authority and Victoria & Albert Museum Circulation Department.

SIDDIG A. EL'NIGOUMI

Born 1931 in the Sudan. After teacher's training in Dilling, West Sudan, worked as calligrapher and illustrator in Publications Bureau at Khartoum, then in 1952 released to take three-year diploma course in arts and crafts at school of art in Khartoum. Studied pottery at Central School of Art and Design, London (1957–60) and returned to teach ceramics at Khartoum school of art. In England from 1967, at first technical assistant and

then teacher at West Surrey College of Art & Design, Farnham; also teaches at Central School and Medway College of Design in Kent. Exhibitions include one man shows in England (1970 and 1973); group exhibitions, e.g. at Design Centre, London; International Ceramics Exhibition at Victoria & Albert Museum (1972), International Ceramics, Faenza, Italy (1972 and 1975); New Grafton Gallery, London (1976).

MARY ROGERS

Born 1929 in Derbyshire. Apprenticed as calligrapher to printer at 16 years old; sent by firm for extra training at St Martin's School of Art, London, and worked for many years as calligrapher and illustrator. After marriage to Bob Rogers, who was then studying sculpture, became interested in working with clay. Studied ceramics and experimented continually, concentrating on methods of modelling and building by hand; set up pottery studio in 1960. Lecturer in ceramics at Loughborough College of Education (1966–70), and has taught part time at several Colleges of Art. Elected exhibiting member, Midlands Group of Artists (1961), Craftsman Potters' Association (1965), British Crafts Centre (1968), International Academy of Ceramics (1972). Work shown in Tokyo (1965), Stockholm (1970), Faenza (1971), Hamburg (1973 and 1974), and Brussels (1973), and in permanent collections of Metropolitan Museum of Art, and Museum of Modern Art, New York, Pennsylvania Museum, USA, Boymans van Beuningen Rotterdam, Holland, British Council and Crafts Advisory Council, museums and art galleries in Bradford, Portsmouth, Swindon, Derby, Leicester, Nottingham and London. Recent exhibitions include one man shows at Oxford Gallery (1974), British Crafts Centre (1975), Midland Gallery, Nottingham (1976); forthcoming shows at Peter Dingley Gallery, Stratford on Avon (1977) and at Oxford Gallery (1978).

PETER STARKEY

Born 1945. Studied fine arts (1963–65) at Portsmouth Art School. Teacher's training at Cardiff College of Education (1967–69) followed by one year's teaching in London. Studio pottery course at Harrow (1971–73). In 1973, established saltglaze pottery at Hunworth, Norfolk, with the help of one of first Crafts Advisory Council workshop grants. Moved to Dartington, Devon, in 1975. Work recently shown at Barclaycraft, the Casson Gallery, and at Heal's in London (1975).

BIOGRAPHIES

GEOFFREY SWINDELL

Born 1945 in Stoke-on-Trent. Studied in Stoke-on-Trent and at the Royal College of Art. Lecturer in charge of ceramics at York School of Art (1970–75); now lectures at Cardiff College of Art. Recent exhibitions include one man shows at Oxford Gallery, Midland Group Gallery, Nottingham, Sutton College, Surrey, 'Towards Ceramic Sculpture' (Oxford Gallery), 'New Ceramics' (British Craft Centre), 'Ceramic Forms' (CAC and British Council—toured Europe), all in 1974; 'Contemporary English Ceramics', Kilkenny, Eire (1975); New members' exhibition, Craftsman Potters' Association (1976).

YEAP POH CHAP

Born 1927 in Malaysia. After work in pottery near Aarhus, Denmark (1961), studied ceramics at Putney Evening Institute, London (1962–63), then at Hammersmith College of Art and Building (1963–66). Research student at Royal College of Art (1967–68), then established own workshop in Surrey. Teacher of ceramics until 1975 at St Paul's School, London. Work shown in group exhibitions at Camden Arts Centre, London ('Artist Craftsmen', 1966); The Royal West of England Academy ('Craftsmanship Today', 1967); Research Exhibition at Royal College of Art (1967–68); 'Oriental Themes' at Grosvenor Gallery (1968). One man shows in 1973, 1974 and 1975 at Brian Koetser Gallery, London. One of six official British entires for Faenza ceramic competition, 1975.